BLACK PATRIOT AND MARTYR

Toussaint of Haiti

BORN: C. 1744
DIED: APRIL 7, 1803

The colony of Haiti, where Toussaint Louverture was born, was the jewel of the French Empire whose prosperity and culture were built upon black labor, a vast slave population held in check by whip and gun. When the shock waves of the French Revolution reached the Caribbean, the time was right for rebellion. Toussaint transformed the rebels into a disciplined army and was invincible both on the battlefields and at the negotiating table. Barbaric betrayal by the French under Napoleon ended his dream of the first black republic, and sent him to a tragic death in a grim fortress prison. The story of a courageous man who fought for the freedom and dignity of every man.

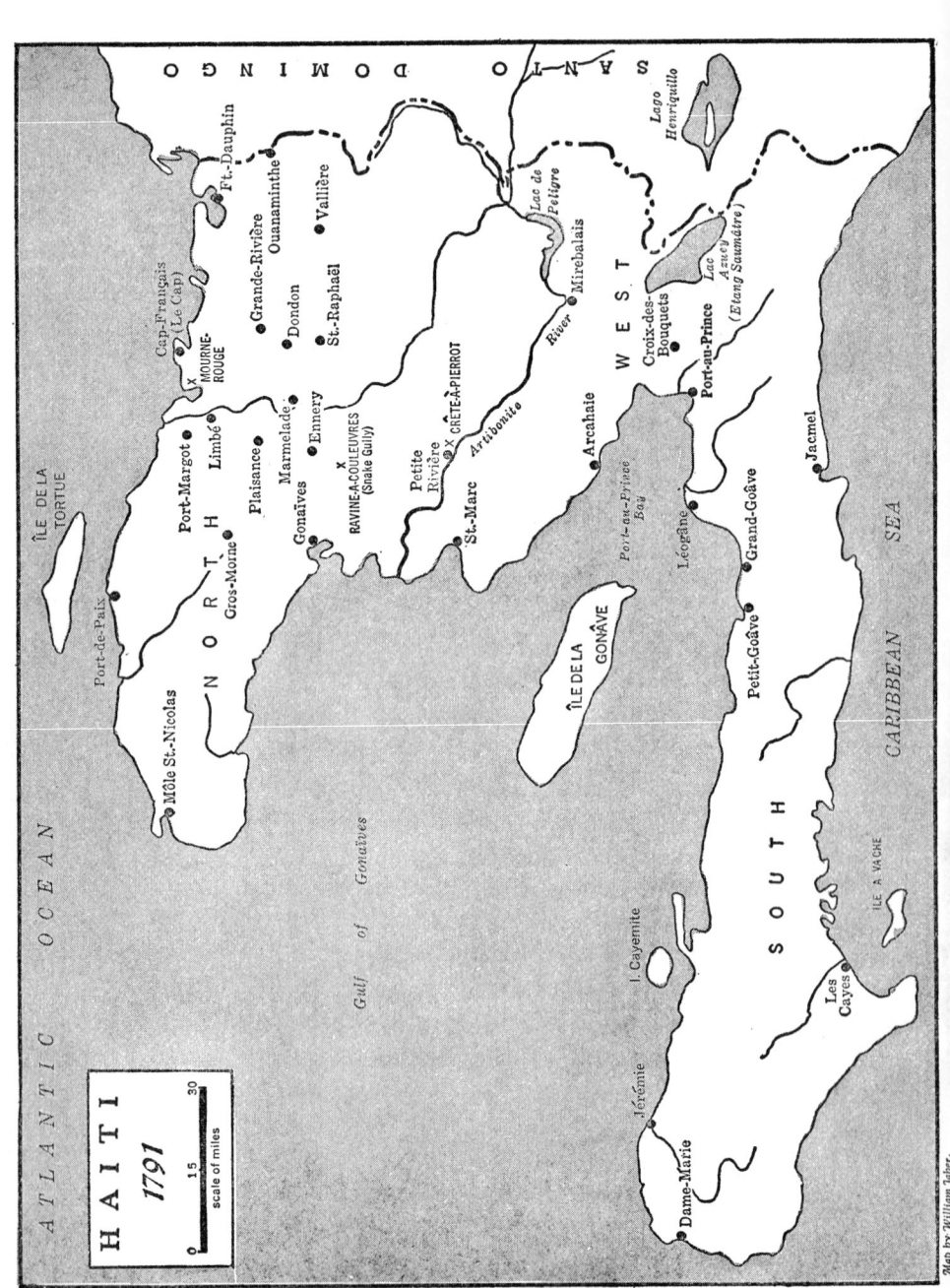

BLACK PATRIOT AND MARTYR
Toussaint of Haiti

by **Ann Griffiths**

JULIAN MESSNER NEW YORK

Published simultaneously in the United States and Canada by Julian Messner, a division of Simon & Schuster, Inc., 1 West 39 Street, New York, N.Y. 10018. All rights reserved.

Copyright, ©, 1970 by Barbara Ann Griffiths

Second Printing, 1972

Printed in the United States of America

ISBN 0-671-32264-8 Cloth Trade
ISBN 0-671-32265-8 MCE

Library of Congress Catalog Card No. 71-107396

PROLOGUE

IT was almost dawn. Soon the relentless tropical sun would station itself in the sky, smothering Haiti with its brutal white heat. But now, the harbor of Le Cap, the colony's capital, was cool, the darkness above the water dotted with the many dim lights of oil lamps swaying softly from invisible masts.

As usual, Le Cap's harbor was filled, for Haiti in 1758 was France's richest colony and one of the wealthiest in the world. Trim little French warships, slave ships just in from Africa, cargo ships from many parts of the world waiting to load up with molasses, sugar, coffee and rum—all rested at anchor, their crews asleep.

Aboard one of the warships, under heavy guard, was an ex-slave named Macandal, a fearless African from Guinea. The whites of Haiti called him the most dangerous man in the colony. In a few hours he was to be burned at the stake.

Onshore two *maréchaussée*, police who hunted down fugitive slaves, kept their eyes trained on the warship. As the first light of morning streaked the sky, they saw the small, dark shape of a rowboat detach itself from the warship and move slowly toward shore. Soon the *maréchaussée* could hear the anxious, muffled voices of French soldiers mingling with the sound of oars dipping in the water. The prisoner Macandal was being brought ashore.

When the rowboat pulled alongside the dock, the two *maréchaussée* rushed forward and yanked the half-naked prisoner out of the boat. Dragging Macandal between them, they ran toward a horse-drawn carriage waiting near the quay, and shoved the prisoner inside. Then they leaped in behind him, slammed the door, and drew the curtains shut. A dozen mounted dragoons appeared out of the shadows and followed the carriage as it sped away from the harbor and through the narrow, deserted streets of Le Cap.

Like all public ceremonies, Macandal's execution was to be held early in the morning, before the blazing sun became intolerable. As the carriage approached the Place de Royale, one of Haiti's most elegant squares, the coachman could see and hear the noisy crowds ahead—tanned Creole (Haitian-born) planters in white linen suits and broad-brimmed straw hats; exotic mulatto women with huge gold earrings and towering headdresses; half-naked slaves; completely naked children of all colors; Frenchmen, Englishmen, Spaniards, Maltese, Italians, Americans, Portuguese—a whole cross section of Haiti's society waited, hot and impatient, in the square.

Macandal was the leader of a large and dangerous band of outlaws and ex-slaves called the Maroons. His plan to free thousands of slaves had failed, but the plot, when uncovered, had struck fear into the heart of white Haiti.

Now, struggling fiercely, his hands bound, the prisoner was led through the mocking crowd toward a tall, empty stake in the middle of the square. It took several strong men to hold him while the chains were bound about his hands and feet. The *maréchaussée* piled small logs and chips of wood at Macandal's feet. The fire was lit, and tiny flames danced out. The crowd stopped chattering, and all eyes were on the victim.

To the audience, this was entertainment. As Macandal twisted and wrenched his body to avoid the softly crackling, death-bearing flames, they guffawed much as they would have at a wrestling match or a circus performance. Dainty Creole ladies stifled snickers, while their escorts laughed openly. A French sailor cheered drunkenly at the prisoner's futile gestures. And the slaves in the audience looked on, helpless and sick.

Writhing in pain, Macandal made a last, superhuman effort to break his chains. A chain burst, and the guffaws of the audience became shouts of horror. For the briefest moment, fear changed sides. Could the blacks be right? Perhaps he *did* possess supernatural powers!

The slaves, forgetting all caution, screamed, "They can't kill you, brother Macandal! Fly! Fly!"

But Macandal's burned body, half-freed from the chains, sagged and collapsed into the flames. His plan to free the slaves died with him.

The fire was out, but the ashes still burned . . .

That night, high on a hill overlooking the sleeping plantations outside Le Cap, a lone African drum began to throb. Soon it was answered by the muffled beat of another drum on a nearby hill, then a third in the valley below, a fourth deep in the mountain forest. All over the hills, dark figures, summoned by the drums, quietly emerged.

The Maroons were gathering. For them and many of the slaves, Macandal was gone, but not dead. One old slave, hearing of his leader's fate, shook his head and said, "Macandal isn't dead. No white man can kill Macandal. He just changed himself into a mosquito and flew away. When the time is right, he'll come back again in human shape and free us all. Just wait. You'll see."

And when the time was right, the spirit of Macandal did come back in human shape—that of Toussaint Louverture, one of the greatest liberators in history.

CHAPTER 1

WHEN Christopher Columbus first saw the mountainous little island in the West Indies just east of Cuba, he could describe it only in superlatives. Already jubilant over his discoveries in the New World, he said on that morning in December, 1492, that he had discovered the "paradise of God" and the "most beautiful thing in the world."

Claiming the island for Spain, Columbus named it Hispaniola, meaning "Little Spain." But the Arawaks, the gentle natives who welcomed Columbus, called their island "Haiti"—"The Land of the Mountains."

It was always summer in Haiti. Year round, from the precipitous mountaintops down to the golden beaches below, a wild exuberance of tropical vegetation covered the land. The many mountains gave rise to numerous pure, cool streams which meandered through the valleys, making the land lush, fertile and green.

So pleased was Columbus with this land and its people that he decided to leave behind a colony before returning to Spain to report his discoveries. Santo Domingo, established on the southeastern coast, became the first place in the New World to be colonized by Europeans.

The colonists of Santo Domingo and their descendants apparently lacked Columbus' appreciation of the gentle Arawaks, for in a short time they massacred or worked to death nearly every last one. Shooting natives became a sport for bored Spanish gentlemen—less exciting than big-game hunting, since the natives were naked and unarmed, but entertaining nevertheless.

Between two and three million Arawaks were living happily in Haiti when the Spaniards arrived. About twenty years later only fourteen thousand remained. Today not a single pure-blooded descendant can be found.

Having exhausted that human supply, the Spaniards turned to Africa. The blacks, physically superior to the Arawaks, proved to be far more suitable as slaves, and by 1510 a regular commerce in slaves between Africa and the New World had begun.

The Spaniards, however, were lazy as well as cruel and more interested in gold than in farming. The colony of Santo Domingo began to languish, and the entire western third of the island of Hispaniola was neglected. Eventually French and English buccaneers roaming the Spanish Main made a little island off the northwest coast their base of operations. From there these pirates would sally forth in their swift little flyboats and attack the stately Spanish galleons carrying treasure from the New World back to Spain.

But a pirate's life was a strenuous one, and many buccaneers, yearning for a steadier way to earn a living, began to settle on Haiti, where they hunted cattle the lackadaisical Spaniards had let run wild. More and more Frenchmen came, forcing the English out, and soon France sent women to help populate the area. Most of these women were the dregs of Paris' courtesans.

The children of the marriages between buccaneers and courtesans became the first Creoles of Haiti. Any white born in Haiti was called a Creole, and many had at least one uncouth French buccaneer or Paris courtesan on their ancestral tree.

In 1697, under the terms of the Treaty of Ryswick, Spain ceded the western third of the island to France, and it became the French colony of Saint Domingue (often called San Domingo or St. Domingo). This French colony became the Haiti of today, while the Spanish colony of Santo Domingo became the Dominican Republic.

Unlike the Spanish, the French were an energetic lot. Three centuries after the arrival of Columbus, his once-wild "paradise of God" resembled an ambitious farmer's dream. Tidy little coffee trees dotted the mountain slopes, and a neat patchwork quilt of plantations covered the valleys and plains. Everywhere, seas of light-green sugarcane rippled in the soft trade winds.

Haiti was the pride of France and the richest colony in the world. Its soil was so fertile and its climate so favorable year-round that sugarcane, coffee beans, cotton, tobacco, indigo, cacao grew in profusion on Haiti's many plantations. And, although no larger than the state of Vermont, the colony exported two thirds of France's total commerce.

Most of Haiti's plantations were owned by Frenchmen and Creoles who grew so rich off the lush, fertile land that "rich as a Creole" became a common saying in Paris. The planters, however, never touched a hoe. The actual source of labor, the structure on which all their wealth rested, was Haiti's half-million slaves.

The Bréda plantation, located on the heights overlooking Le Cap and the blue-green sea, was one of the most beautiful in the colony. Its cane fields, bounded by green, well-trimmed hedges, stretched as far as the eye could see. A long road, lined with tall, graceful palm trees led up to the large white plantation house. The mansion was shaded by wide verandas and groves of banana trees. From the gardens came the heavy scent of jasmine, honeysuckle and orange blossom.

Beyond the house was the stable, and farther away, well out of sight of the mansion, were the huddled rows of little thatched huts, home of Bréda's one thousand slaves.

It was here, on All Saint's Day about the year 1744, that François Dominique Toussaint was born. He was, according to custom, surnamed after his plantation and called Toussaint Bréda. Years later Toussaint adopted the name Louverture, the French word for "opening," after a French general, flabbergasted at Toussaint's military successes, had exclaimed, "That man makes an opening wherever he goes!"

Toussaint was so sickly when born that his parents did not expect him to live. And when he grew older, he was still so skinny his friends made fun of him, calling out, *"fatras-bâton!"* meaning "little stick."

But Toussaint made up in pride and self-discipline what he lacked in strength. Every day he spent hours doing strenuous exercises, forcing his frail body to the limits of its endurance. By the time he was twelve, he was the athletic superior of all the other slaves his age at Bréda.

Toussaint's father, Gaou-Ginou, was the proud son of a West African chieftain. Captured during a tribal war, he was taken by his enemies to Dahomey, sold as a slave and packed into the stinking hold of a slave ship bound for Haiti. By the time the journey was over, the ship was little more than a huge coffin floating on the surface of the sea.

Once in Haiti, the slaves were worked like animals, housed like animals, starved, beaten and cowed into docility, until they died of humiliation, pain and fatigue. For the least fault they were whipped. For a serious fault they might be whipped to death. As an example to frighten other slaves, or perhaps just to amuse themselves, the masters often devised new and more twisted means of torture.

Slaves were roasted over a slow fire, tossed into boiling cauldrons of sugar, stuffed with gunpowder and blown up with a match, buried up to their necks and smeared with molasses so the flies would devour them slowly, or mutilated, limb by limb.

Haiti's was a vicious society. Brutality, far from being considered criminal or depraved, was socially acceptable. But some of the slaves were more fortunate than others. Gaou-Ginou, Toussaint's father, was one of them.

At Bréda, where Gaou-Ginou lived, the sound of the whip was seldom heard. The Count de Bréda, who owned the plantation, had ordered that his slaves be treated humanely, and "as lucky as a Bréda slave" was a common saying among slaves on other plantations.

Gaou-Ginou's master recognized the superior bearing of his slave, and gave him many privileges and a plot of land of his own to farm. He married another Bréda slave, a beautiful black woman named Pauline, and had eight children, the first of whom was Toussaint.

Gaou-Ginou taught his son much about the ways of Africa. Toussaint learned the Arada language, spoken by his father's tribe, and how to recognize and use medicinal herbs. The Arada tribe was famous for its warriors, and Toussaint learned much about the art of guerrilla warfare from his father's vivid tales of tribal wars.

Because his father was a leader among the slaves and respected by the whites of Bréda, Toussaint was well treated. Most slaves lived in small, windowless palm-thatched huts made of mud and wattle, with a beaten earth floor. Toussaint's hut was larger than most, and relatively light and airy. And, unlike most slaves, even those at Bréda, he seldom went hungry.

On the plantation was another unusual man. Pierre Baptiste, a full-blooded Negro of the Arada tribe, had been given his freedom after many years of hard work. He was also given a plot of land at Bréda, and he continued to live there, farming his land. His previous owners, Jesuit fathers, had taught him to read and write, and converted him to Catholicism. His name was known and respected by blacks for miles around.

Pierre Baptiste was Toussaint's godfather. On Sundays, the one day slaves had any free time, he would take Toussaint for long walks. "Slavery dulls the body and the mind," he warned the young boy. Pointing to the slaves squatting in front of their huts, he said, "Look at them. Look at the blank expressions on their faces. They sit there for hours, just staring vacantly into space. All they look forward to is death. They think if they die, they'll wake up in Africa."

Toussaint's godfather shook his head sadly. "They'll never see Africa again. And you, my son, will never see Africa at all. *This* is your home. Bréda is your home. But you're very lucky. Here, if you act smart and work very hard, someday, many years from now, you too may win your freedom."

Pierre Baptiste taught Toussaint to speak French and to read and write, skills that set him far ahead of most slaves, who could do neither. Among themselves the slaves generally spoke their tribal tongue. But nearly all knew the Creole language, which was a corrupted form of French. Toussaint even learned a bit of Latin. Occasionally he would indulge in a little showmanship, watching with delight the expression on a friend's face as he awed him with a sonorous liturgical phrase.

But Toussaint was not a playful boy. Quiet and thoughtful almost to the point of melancholy, he took everything very seriously. The death of his mother when he was still young caused him great sorrow. Being the eldest child, he had to bear much of the responsibility for his younger brothers and sisters until his father married again. His stepmother, Pélagie, was good to him, and he learned to love her.

Like many planters, the Count de Bréda returned to France to live, leaving his plantation in the hands of a manager, Bayon de Libertas, a good man who conscientiously obeyed the Count's orders to treat the slaves humanely. He was also a perceptive man who recognized Toussaint's unusual maturity and intelligence.

When Toussaint reached his teens, Monsieur de Libertas gave him the job of guarding the cattle. Sitting day after day on the quiet hills watching the lazy, munching herds, the young slave had plenty of time to think and read. The manager of Bréda, much to the horror of neighboring planters, saw no danger in letting slaves read books, and he even lent Toussaint some of his own. The young slave also borrowed books from the parish priest; Pierre Baptiste had seen to it that his godson was baptized in the Catholic faith.

All in all, life for the young Toussaint was relatively tolerable. But no slave was spared all the sordid consequences of slavery. His favorite sister, Genevieve, though still a child, was sold to a planter in another province. And when Toussaint was about fourteen, Macandal was burned at the stake. He hated violence, and was not at the execution. But like the other slaves, he heard a vivid report. It was a story few slaves could forget. Although Toussaint hated and feared no one, the colony itself was seething with hate and fear.

With Macandal's death, most of the blacks retreated into brooding passivity. Some of the bolder ones plotted and planned. Every now and then there was a minor uprising. But these were quickly crushed and the leaders killed.

As for young Toussaint, life went quietly by. When he was eighteen his love for horses so impressed Monsieur de Libertas that he put Toussaint in charge of the stable. The whites of Bréda trusted and respected this bright, dependable slave, and he in turn seemed to harbor no hatred toward them.

His fellow slaves also held him in high regard. And as this

respect increased over the years, the black who was destined to become "more than just a man—a nation" felt a growing sense of responsibility toward his own people, whose suffering caused him such pain.

CHAPTER 2

"A BLACK—even if he descended from the Magi who bore gifts to the Savior, even if he had the genius of a celestial intelligence and all the gold in the world—would never be anything in the eyes of the poorest, most stupid, most contemptible white in Haiti!" So commented an amazed visitor after a few weeks in the colony.

To survive in such a society, the blacks had to become masters of deception. Even at Bréda a slave didn't dare act too smart. No white could afford to have a slave who was smarter than he.

It was important to the whites to make the blacks believe they were stupid and inferior. A slave who knew he was smart was difficult to humiliate and control. When a colonist wrote in one of his books that "no species of man has more intelligence than the blacks," both the colonist and his book were banned from the colony.

So the blacks hid their true selves from the whites, going through each day with blank, expressionless masks on their faces. They were quiet and obedient, seeing nothing, hearing nothing—just as docile as their masters wanted them to be.

As Toussaint grew into manhood, he too became crafty, hiding the complexities of his personality under the mask of the trustworthy, dependable slave. He early learned to choose his words carefully, rather than blurt out what he really thought.

The whites thought they knew Toussaint. But the real Toussaint was locked up tight, and no white had the key.

When Toussaint reached his thirties, Monsieur de Libertas made him his personal coachman. The two frequently drove to Le Cap, with Toussaint high on the coachman's seat, his handsome uniform braided with gold, but his feet, like those of all slaves, bare.

Toussaint was not handsome or dashing. He was only about five feet two inches tall. His nose was broad, his jaw forbidding. He wore his hair brushed back from his forehead into a pigtail, and often covered his head with a madras handkerchief. But he was powerfully built, lean and wiry, and his bearing was proud and dignified. He rarely smiled, and never raised his voice, but any fellow slave who incurred his displeasure found himself withering under the steely look in Toussaint's piercing black eyes.

Aloof, withdrawn and impenetrable on the surface, he was actually a benevolent man of simple and kindly feelings, incapable of doing anything mean, petty or vindictive.

As coachman to the manager of Bréda, Toussaint became very familiar with Le Cap. The "Paris of the Antilles" was much like the Creole ladies who lived there—charming and lovely if you didn't look too closely, cruel and decadent if you did. Nestled at the foot of the mountains, it was a gaily colored, well-built little city set between the blue waters of the bay and the green hills that rose sharply from behind. It was constructed almost entirely of stone, with tree-lined public squares, graceful fountains, pastel-colored houses and theaters that performed plays by Molière, the latest Italian operas and recent works of the Parisian stage.

Toussaint often had to wait long hours in Le Cap while his master completed his business. This gave him a chance to observe the whites and to mingle with other slaves waiting for their masters. Many of the slaves he talked to belonged to Creoles, and the more he learned of the Creoles, the more fortunate he realized he was.

The richest Creoles in Haiti were the plantation owners. Toussaint saw many of these haughty planters striding about Le Cap—tall, tanned and handsome, immaculately dressed in white linen suits and straw hats, often with a lovely mulatto lady on their arm. The typical Creole planter was courageous, generous and hospitable. He was also proud, quarrelsome and cruel. His ferocious temper was matched only by his wife's. While his manager and overseer ran the plantation, he idled away his life drinking, playing cards and pursuing women.

There were few schools in Haiti, and most Creoles were educated in France, which they regarded as their real home. Haiti's monotonous climate and lack of sophistication bored them. They were far more eager to get rich enough to live in Paris than to make their life in Haiti agreeable. Their mansions, though often elegant on the outside, were crude and uncomfortable inside. The furniture was imported from France, but little care was taken to arrange it in a cozy or tasteful fashion. All the rooms had the temporary air of a hotel, lived in by people who never put down roots.

The Creole woman, with her dark, glossy hair and ivory skin, was a delight to look at until overeating and a too-sedentary life turned her plump and older than her years. Lazy and empty-headed, she spent most of her day stretched out in a hammock or on a divan. Slave girls fanned her, tickled the soles of her feet with a feather and sang the risqué songs she requested. When angered she turned into a spitfire, pinching, slapping, spitting and hurling offensive language at the object of her wrath. She was even more cruel to her slaves than was her husband, and she despised the beautiful mulatto women whom the Creole men found so irresistible.

From the tales related to him by other slaves, Toussaint also learned that the Creoles, despite their wealth, were miserable. The unchanging seasons and the relentless, almost unsupportable heat depressed them. With slaves to do all the work, time hung heavily on their hands. Books were rare, and they wouldn't have read them anyway. In some parts of Haiti plantations were so isolated that the planters seldom saw their neighbors.

Worse than the tedium of their barren lives was the fear. With only about thirty-five thousand whites in a colony with a half-million slaves, the whites lived in a constant state of anxiety.

Toussaint returned from his trips to Le Cap more thoughtful and melancholy than usual. The picture of Haiti that he was piecing together in his mind was like that of a badly built house, balancing precariously on a rotten foundation of fear, hate and greed. He could see, too, that the feelings of hatred and fear were growing stronger, forcing both whites and blacks to ever more horrible excesses.

But back at Bréda the rest of Haiti seemed far away, and Toussaint went about his duties, suppressing painful thoughts about things a simple slave could never change.

Toussaint did not marry until he was about forty years old. In this, as in all else, he displayed his independence. Everyone, including Monsieur de Libertas, tried to persuade him to marry one of the beautiful young slaves on the plantation. But the woman Toussaint finally selected for a wife was neither young nor beautiful.

A relative of Toussaint's godfather, Suzanne Simon was a somewhat plump woman, only five years younger than Toussaint and already a widow with a son. But she had a strong character and a good disposition, and that, Toussaint decided, was more important than physical beauty. Suzanne bore him two sons, Isaac and Saint-Jean, and he never made any distinction between them and his stepson, Placide, treating them all with equal affection.

Monsieur de Libertas eventually made Toussaint steward of all the livestock, a rare position for a slave to hold. Under his stewardship Bréda became the most prosperous plantation in the Northern Province. (Haiti was divided into three provinces—North, West and South.) Rewarded with all the privileges of a freedman, Toussaint was paid a salary and given his own plot of land, which he worked on shares.

Already many slaves looked to Toussaint as their natural leader. At night, when he took long walks by himself, the slaves who saw him go by, lost in thought, would whisper to each other, "He is in communication with the gods."

Toussaint read everything he could get his hands on. He became acquainted with classic military strategy and the art of politics by reading Caesar's Commentaries. The works of Epictetus, a white man enslaved by the Romans, convinced him that a man who remained true to his own values, who knew who he was and respected what he was, would always be free.

Of all the works he read, Toussaint was most impressed by a long history of the West Indies by Abbé Raynal, a French priest who had visited the West Indies and seen the horrors of slavery. Toussaint read the book several times, and was especially impressed by one passage:

> Nations of Europe, your slaves will break the yoke that weighs on them. The blacks lack only a courageous chief. Where is he? Where is that great man to be found? He will appear, do not doubt it. He will raise the sacred standard of liberty and gather round him his companions in misfortune. More impetuous than the mountain torrents, they will leave behind them on all sides the ineffaceable signs of their resent-

ment! The old world as well as the new will applaud him. The name of the hero who will have re-established the rights of the human race will be blessed forever.

In his mind Toussaint turned the questions over and over. "Where is he? Where is that great man to be found?"

Unknown to Toussaint, many others were pondering similar questions, for the stirrings of revolution were in the air. The American colonies had fought for and won their independence from England, and in France the spirit of revolution was on the rise.

As the slaves sweated away in the fields of Haiti and France's profits from the colony soared higher, the French monarchy was drawing closer and closer to its doom.

Early in September of 1789 a French cargo ship dropped anchor in Le Cap's harbor, and its captain rushed ashore, bursting with the news from France.

"The people have rebelled! They have stormed the Bastille! All Paris is in arms!"

The French peasants had finally risen up against their oppressors. The great French Revolution had begun. Europe would never be the same again. Nor would the little colony of Haiti, where the news was to have far-reaching effects on all the people—first the whites, then the mulattoes and, finally, the blacks.

The captain was followed ashore by his sailors, excitedly chattering slogans new to the Haitians' ears—phrases such as "Rights of Man" and "Liberty, Equality and Fraternity." Some sailors, carried away with revolutionary fervor, rushed up to the mystified slaves shouting, "You're free! You're free!"

Many slaves, believing the sailors, began dancing and singing in the streets. Their celebration was short-lived. The next few days witnessed even more than the usual number of executions and murders, as the masters of Haiti came down hard on any slave entertaining such a foolish notion. The news of the Revolution had reached Haiti, but it was to be a while before the Revolution itself arrived.

Toussaint was delighted with events in France, but he had no illusions about liberty. He was certain emancipation was a long way off—in fact he did not expect to see it in his lifetime. But with all the talk about the rights of man, he was sure the slaves would not be forgotten altogether. Perhaps now France would at least enforce the Black Code, laws designed to protect slaves from excessive brutality, laws that almost all slaveowners in Haiti ignored.

As steward of Bréda, Toussaint was freer then ever to travel and to mingle with other blacks. He quickly learned the French Revolution had thrown Haiti into a turmoil.

Among the colonists of Haiti, as in the thirteen colonies before the American Revolution, there was much resentment against the mother country. The colony was ruled by a governor and an officer called an intendant, both appointed by the King of France, Louis XVI. The colonists themselves had no say in the governing of the colony, and were forced to trade exclusively with France. They resented being ruled by the French government, which was so far away and which, they felt, interfered with the proper development of their commercial and agricultural interests. They demanded freedom of commerce, but their demands were ignored. The American Revolution put new ideas into their heads, and after the thirteen colonies became free, many of Haiti's colonists began yearning for independence.

Now there was a new revolution. At first most of the colonists welcomed the French Revolution. Here, they thought, is an opportunity to present our grievances and win some self-rule for the colony. They demanded, and got, representation in the National Assembly, France's new governing body. Then they demanded a say in the running of Haiti, and a representative Colonial Assembly was formed in the colony.

The colonists were delighted with their success. But then the mulattoes of Haiti made their bid for liberty and equality, and shock and horror replaced the enthusiastic applause. Not for a moment had the colonists considered that such rights extended beyond whites.

In Haiti the color of the skin, the varying shades of dark and light, took precedence over all other distinctions, including honor, birth and even fortune. A debauched, illiterate tavernkeeper could be more respected than a wealthy Paris-educated planter if the tavernkeeper were white and the planter, with black blood in his veins, a mulatto.

Haiti had almost as many mulattoes as whites. Most were free, and many owned slaves. There was no law against mulattoes accumulating riches, and they owned a considerable part of Haiti's wealth, often living in handsome estates or on beautiful plantations. They sent their sons to school in Paris, and on the whole they were more sophisticated and cultured than the Creoles. But the social standing of the mulattoes depended on neither their wealth nor their sophistication, but solely on how much white blood they had in their veins. Even when they were accepted socially, they were subject to the most outrageous kinds of discrimination. There was one kind of justice for whites and another kind for mulattoes.

For those mulattoes who had been educated in Paris, where whites treated them as equals, this discrimination was especially galling. The "Little Whites" of Haiti were a special torment to them.

The Little Whites were all those whites who didn't fit into the category of "Big Whites," a group that included the wealthy planters, merchants and high French officials. Shopkeepers, barbers, clerks, artisans and small plantation owners with only a few slaves, as well as fortune-seeking adventurers, debtors on the run, fugitives from justice and unsavory underworld types from every imaginable place formed Haiti's class of Little Whites.

The Little White was the true aristocrat of the skin. No matter how much of a failure he had been, no matter how many crimes he had committed before coming to the colony, in Haiti he was a man of stature. He was *white*.

Toussaint could not avoid these puffed-up Little Whites, who were everywhere in Le Cap. But he had too much self-respect to let them ruffle his dignity. If one insulted him, he pretended he didn't hear. He knew answering back meant death. Why risk his life on someone so obviously his inferior? After all, strip away his white skin and he would be nothing—a man with little or no education, with no sense of honor or concept justice.

The Little Whites fought even more feverishly than the Big Whites to retain the discriminatory status quo. And the status quo did *not* include equal rights for mulattoes.

The mulattoes had other ideas. Tired of being discriminated against, they decided to test the revolutionary sincerity of France. They sent a delegation to the National Assembly to present their grievances.

When the whites of Haiti learned the National Assembly had accepted the mulatto delegation, they were beside themselves with fury. Whereas before the mulattoes were just treated unjustly, now, everywhere in Haiti, they were terrorized and even lynched. Finally, they were pushed too far. Vincent Ogé, a well-educated and wealthy mulatto, organized an insurrection.

Toussaint did not learn of the mulatto uprising until it

was over, until the mulatto rebels had been slaughtered and Ogé broken on the wheel. More than thirty years had passed since Macandal had failed and been burned at the stake. Since then the minor slave uprisings had all been squelched immediately and with ease, and now the mulatto revolt had been snuffed out.

Toussaint was convinced more than ever of the futility of rebelling. The blacks had no arms, no organization, no leader. If they rebelled, they would be massacred just like the mulattoes. Were the blacks and mulattoes to unite against the whites, there might be some hope. But the mulattoes and blacks were as divided as ever. The uprising had proven that.

A group in Paris called the Friends of the Blacks had given Ogé money and arms. The Friends of the Blacks, probably the first group of its kind ever organized, was made up of people who wanted to abolish slavery and discrimination. But Ogé was concerned only with his own people, and he did not call the slaves to arms. If he had, his revolt might have succeeded. Unfortunately, the mulattoes, themselves the victims of discrimination, looked down on and despised the blacks.

Ogé dead was far more effective to the mulatto cause than Ogé alive. News of his martyrdom created a storm in Paris and in Haiti. Mulattoes everywhere and decent whites all over France demanded action. The French government responded. It passed a decree giving mulattoes equal rights, and sent three commissioners to Haiti to see that the decree was carried out.

When the commissioners landed in Haiti, they found the colony in ferment. The whites and mulattoes were at each other's throats, the supporters of the French Revolution were pitted against the supporters of the monarchy (the royalists), and many colonists were screaming for independence from France. The colony was close to an out-and-out revolt against the mother country, and the French bureaucrats who ruled Haiti were at their wit's end. So busy were the whites fighting among themselves and with the mulattoes, they never stopped to wonder what the slaves were thinking.

The tumult was so great even peaceful Bréda felt the tremors. At evening meals the white-robed house slaves waited silently on their masters, one behind each chair. Their expressions typically impassive, they showed not the slightest sign of hearing or comprehending the conversations of the whites. But at night the slave quarters buzzed with excitement, as the blacks related what they had overheard.

The French Revolution, all the talk of liberty and equality, Ogé's uprising, the decree granting mulattoes equal rights, the colonists demanding independence—every detail was discussed and argued over. What did it all mean? Was there hope for the slaves? Perhaps now was the time to make a move. . . .

Toussaint gave his opinions, and, as usual, the blacks listened with respect. "We must be patient," the leader of Bréda's slaves cautioned. "France is making great strides toward the ideals of liberty and equality. The slaves cannot be ignored much longer. It is just a matter of time now before our grievances will be heard."

Other slaves—men less intellectual and more emotional than Toussaint—had different ideas. They had no faith in France, and felt the time was right. But they had learned an important lesson from Ogé's uprising. They dare not fail. It was essential to organize and unite.

Once again the African drums began to beat more frequently. But white Haiti was now so distracted by all the internal squabbling that they just assumed the drums were, as usual, calling the slaves to one of their African rituals. They did not hear the new note of warning in the steady, ominous beat-beat from the hills. They did not hear the drums summoning the blacks to arise.

CHAPTER 3

THE night of August 14, 1791, was hot and sultry. A tropical storm threatened. In the thick pine forests covering the Morne-Rouge, a mountain overlooking Le Cap, the air was heavy and still; all the forest waited in hushed silence for the dreaded fury of the storm about to break.

The blacks threading their way along the mountain trails saw lightning and heard spasms of thunder in the distance. When they reached their destination, the Bois Caïman glade, they found the clearing lit with smoking torches. On a large rock, his skin glistening in the torchlight, sat a Maroon. Between his legs was a drum about four feet high with black goatskin pegged across the top. Although the blacks had heard the drum clearly a mile away, its beat, as they stood next to the drum, was indistinct and low.

About two hundred slaves, all foremen of slave gangs that worked in the fields, were seated in a half circle. They had come from some one hundred different plantations in the Northern Province, and had spent much of this, their one day off, walking to the Bois Caïman. Standing in their midst, wearing a long red robe and holding a burning torch in his hand, was a voodoo high priest, a tall and commanding Jamaican named Boukman, giving the blacks their final instructions.

Boukman's plan was far more grandiose than Macandal's. *All* the blacks in Haiti—not just thousands in the Northern Province—were to be freed.

After plans for the uprising had been settled, the voodoo ritual began. Toward the edge of the glade was an altar with the image of a serpent carved on it. Damballa, bringer of rain, was one of the important voodoo gods, and the serpent her symbol. A live pig lay on top of the altar, its feet tied. Beside the altar stood a tall voodoo priestess. When Boukman gave her a sign, she picked up a long knife and held it above her head, gleaming in the torchlight. Thunder rumbled through the forest, and the blacks sat in silence. The priestess plunged the knife into the pig, and several blacks rushed forward with vessels to catch the blood. Rum and gunpowder were added to the blood, and the vessels passed from hand to hand.

As the blacks drank, they swayed slowly back and forth, the light of the torches dancing on their naked chests, and chanted in African an oath against the whites.

Voodooism, the African cult of nature and ancestor worship, was the true religion of most of Haiti's blacks. Like all religions, it was a set of practices and beliefs to help them deal with the forces of the universe. For the blacks of Haiti, voodooism was more than religious consolation. It was their medium of conspiracy, and the voodoo drums their equivalent of an underground wireless system through which the blacks communicated with each other. The whites had long ago stopped trying to prevent the voodoo rituals, which they had decided were harmless, and the drums did not arouse their suspicion. Why the sound still made them uncomfortable, they did not know.

By daybreak all the blacks who had attended the meeting in the Bois Caïman were back at their plantations. They went about their duties like ordinary slaves, betraying no sign of the fears and hopes stirring in their hearts.

Toussaint was not at the meeting in the glade, for as a devout Catholic he disdained voodooism and its rituals. But he learned of Boukman's plan, and he feared for the blacks. The time, he felt, was not right.

Education had made Toussaint less impulsive about life than most of the slaves. He would prefer to see reforms carried out peacefully, without violence. He did not want to kill. He felt he could never kill his master. And he was convinced the blacks who rebelled would all be slaughtered, just as the mulattoes had been.

The cautious Toussaint persuaded the slaves on Bréda to be patient, to remain aloof from Boukman's plan. But there were thousands of other slaves in Haiti with no one like Toussaint to caution them to wait.

About one week after the meeting in Bois Caïman, in the Northern Province of Haiti, night turned into day. The people of Le Cap, rushing into the streets, saw on the horizon beyond their city a monstrous wall of flames. The Northern Plain, one of the richest agricultural areas in the world, was on fire. The burning cane straw, caught up by the wind, blew down over Le Cap, its crimson rain obscuring the moon and stars. Little fires started all over the city, and as the people rushed from place to place struggling to extinguish them, they did not say it, but in their hearts they knew: the insurrection had begun.

The blacks had followed Boukman's instructions faithfully. At the designated time gang foremen on every plantation in the North except Bréda had led all the slaves out of their quarters. They carried machetes, spades, sticks whittled to a sharp end—anything they could find to serve as a weapon. Even the children carried little sticks.

Exulting in their first taste of liberty, the slaves ran around the plantations shouting "Vengeance! Vengeance!" and "Destroy the whites!"

At first the rebellion was surprisingly moderate. Except for especially detested masters, only those whites who tried to stop the rebels were killed. But the blacks had been treated too badly for too long, and the fever of revenge began to take hold. The masters who had shown the slaves how to hate, humiliate and murder now became victims of their own example. Whites were slaughtered by the hundreds—men, women and children alike. Everything that belonged to the whites was destroyed.

Many whites fled to Le Cap, which was protected by a strong militia and the guns of the French warships in the harbor. Bayon de Libertas, Bréda's manager, had been in the city on business when the insurrection began. Now, with slaves roaming over the countryside, a white man's life was worth little on the open road. Forced to remain in the city, Monsieur de Libertas could only trust that Toussaint would protect Bréda and his wife.

As soon as the news of the rebellion had reached Bréda, Madame de Libertas, almost hysterical with fear, rushed to her steward and dependable slave. "Toussaint, don't abandon me, I beg you! You must save Bréda! You must help me!"

Toussaint took charge of the whole plantation. While the rebellion roared in the distance like an angry sea, Bréda was calm. The plantation's slaves were confused by Toussaint's refusal to join the revolt, but their respect for him was so great they obeyed him and stayed. Their lives went on much as before, only now Toussaint, not Monsieur de Libertas, gave them their instructions.

Three weeks went by, and still the insurrection raged. The whites, who had been taken by surprise, were now organizing. Most of the mulattoes sided with the whites against the rebels, and French soldiers and armed mulattoes and whites either shot all blacks on sight or subjected them to fiendish tortures. Many of the slaves who had not rebelled were so terrified by the murderous and indiscriminatory policy of the whites that they fled to the rebel camps for protection.

A Creole planter was asked by a visitor why the blacks were rebelling. "Oh, they keep mumbling something about the rights of man and equality," he replied irritably. "They don't know *what* they're fighting for!"

But the blacks did know, and soon one hundred thousand slaves—one-fifth of Haiti's total slave population—were in revolt.

It was the most massive uprising in Haiti's history, and still Toussaint hesitated. Everything in him cried out against the orgy of bloodshed, violence and destruction. If he joined, he would imperil the lives of Bréda's one thousand slaves, since they were certain to follow him. And then there was his family to think about.

Toussaint was now about forty-seven. Because of the life they led, slaves aged early, and Toussaint did not think of himself as young. He had a position of unparalleled responsibility for a slave, an income and a relatively secure and comfortable life. If he joined the revolt, he would be leaving behind everything he had worked so hard for all his life. Other slaves did not have nearly as much to lose by becoming rebels.

Toussaint still felt the uprising would not succeed. Although most of the Northern Province was in the hands of the blacks, the other provinces had not rebelled and the whites still controlled Le Cap. Most of the rebels had united and set up camps in the hills, but many still roamed over the hills in small bands, killing and stealing haphazardly. The rebellion had no real organization or direction.

Toussaint did not sleep well these days. More and more rebels kept appearing at the plantation, urging the slaves to join them. The slaves of Bréda grew restless.

Then news reached Bréda that Boukman, the rebel leader, had been killed. The whites had thrown up a strong cordon around the Northern Province to prevent the insurrection from spreading, and the rebels were confined to the Northern Plain.

Once one of the richest agricultural areas in the world, the Northern Plain should have yielded the rebels an abundance of food. But Boukman lacked Toussaint's intellect and foresight.

He was a courageous man, but he had not looked ahead. In their orgy of destruction, the rebels had reduced the plains to a scorched wasteland—one thousand sugar, coffee, cotton and other plantations burned to the ground. With all the crops destroyed, the rebels had nothing to eat. They were hungry, tired and confused. The women and children especially were growing weak from lack of food.

The rebels needed a leader. Once again the question returned to Toussaint's mind: "Where is he? Where is that great man to be found?"

As Toussaint pondered through the sleepless nights, a decision began to form in his mind—a decision that would change the course of Haiti's history and spell disaster to French colonialism in the New World.

One morning, four weeks after the uprising had begun, Toussaint woke his wife and said, "Get yourself and my sons ready." Suzanne understood. She arose and began preparing for the trip across the border. Toussaint then headed toward the plantation house. He found Madame de Libertas seated alone at a long, heavy mahogany table in the dining room. To Toussaint she looked very small and helpless. He knew that without him her life was worth nothing.

When he spoke, his voice was gentle. "Mistress, I can no longer be responsible for you here. Every day more and more rebels come by, urging my brothers to follow them. The Bréda slaves will not stay much longer. Alone I cannot guarantee your protection. Most of the rebels know and respect me, but there are many who do not, and . . ."

"You're right, Toussaint," Madame de Libertas interrupted him. "We can stay here no longer. We'll join Monsieur de Libertas in Le Cap. No harm will come to me on the road with you and your family along."

Toussaint knew if he fled to Le Cap with Madame de Libertas and his family, his comfort would be guaranteed for as long as he lived. Slowly he shook his head. "No, mistress. My people need me now. I will help you pack, and my brother Paul will escort you to Le Cap. With him you'll be safe. My family will go over the border into Santo Domingo. After that I must join the rebel forces."

Madame de Libertas looked at the dependable slave who was now defying her. His voice was soft and gentle, but his eyes were cold, colder than she had ever seen them.

Toussaint's younger brother Paul drove the carriage up to the house, and the slaves loaded it with their mistress' possessions. Toussaint helped the weeping Madame de Libertas into the carriage, reassuring her again.

He then bid her good-bye, and watched as the carriage rode down the long road leading out of the plantation. Madame de Libertas reached Le Cap safely, and she and her husband soon departed for France. Years later, when peace returned to the colony, their former slave sent them the revenue from Bréda, which, out of respect for Toussaint, the rebels did not burn.

Toussaint waited until dark before leaving with his family and Pierre Baptiste, now an old man and nearly blind. He knew Madame de Libertas was safer on the road than he. The whites would certainly not harm her, and, with his brother Paul along, neither would the rebels. But the whites would shoot Toussaint and his family on sight.

The slaves of Bréda gathered around Toussaint, and he gave them their instructions. "Stay together until you get to the rebel camp. Travel by night and keep off the roads. The militia has orders to shoot all blacks on sight. Toussaint will join you again at the camp."

Toussaint helped his family into one of Bréda's carriages,

bid the slaves farewell, and set out on the long, dangerous journey to the border. His family would be safe in Santo Domingo. The sleepy Spanish colony had very few slaves compared to Haiti, and much of it was isolated.

At the border Toussaint said good-bye to his family, knowing he might never see them again, and mounted one of the horses that had pulled the carriage. He then rode at top speed back to the hills of Haiti's Northern Province, keeping a careful eye out for whites and especially the dreaded militia.

The sight of the rebel camp shocked Toussaint, and the army he had come to join seemed piteous to his eyes. The blacks were dressed in filthy rags or ridiculous silks and brocades stolen from their masters' and mistresses' wardrobes. Many wore only loincloths, and some were naked. Sanitary conditions were sickening, and the wounded were being cared for by voodoo priests and medicine men. For weapons they had only machetes and other agricultural tools, iron-pointed sticks, old rusty swords and some muskets stolen from the whites. The "cavalry" was a band of half-naked blacks mounted on worn-out old mules or draft and saddle horses.

Three self-styled leaders had taken Boukman's place. Jean-François was a young Haitian-born slave who had escaped from his plantation and joined the Maroons before the uprising. Powerfully built, with handsome, even features, he had a strange, almost wild glitter in his eyes that disturbed Toussaint. Although an intelligent man, Jean-François had little military ability beyond an extreme tenacity which refused to admit defeat. Biassou was an ugly man with a coarse personality and explosive temper, especially when he was drunk, which was quite frequently. But he had more military ability than Jean-François. The third leader, Jeannot, had been treated so badly as a slave it had turned him into a brute, obsessed with a fanatical hatred toward whites and a raging desire for revenge.

He committed such barbarous atrocities against the whites that he shocked the other rebels.

All three were courageous to the point of recklessness. They loved to dominate, were jealous of their power and put their own interests well ahead of those of their people. Oblivious to the desperate condition of their pathetic little army, they endowed themselves with titles and strutted about the camp dressed in military finery stolen from plantations.

All three were bewildered. They would not admit it, but Toussaint could see they were lost. Cordoned off on all sides, with no source of food or supplies, they did not know what to do next.

Toussaint's arrival put them on their guard. They were not about to share their authority with anyone, much less someone who had been friendly with whites. Nor did they like the warm reception their men had given Toussaint. The three leaders went into a hasty conference. Having learned that Toussaint had a knowledge of medicinal herbs, they decided to make him physician to the army.

Toussaint wisely accepted the post, and in a short time had the camp cleaned up and sanitary and medical conditions improved. Each day he made his way through the camp, binding wounds, administering herbs to the sick and reassuring all with his confident, gentle manner. The rebels respected this man who took no fancy title, wore no fancy uniform, but was always concerned and ready to help anyone who needed it. He was not aggressive with his advice, but his wisdom, his knowledge of military strategy and his natural qualities of leadership were obvious. Soon even Biassou and Jean-François found themselves coming to him for advice.

As his influence over the two leaders grew, Toussaint managed to convince them that Jeannot's barbarous atrocities must stop. Jeannot had taken to decorating his section of the camp with pikes topped by severed heads. Other rebels told Toussaint that Jeannot even drank the blood of his victims, murmuring "Ah, how good this white blood. Let's all quench our thirst and swear revenge!"

It sickened Toussaint to see a leader of his people act as monstrous as the white master who had destroyed his mind. "The thirst for revenge is destroying our cause," Toussaint admonished the rebel leaders.

Jeannot was warned. When, after several warnings, he continued his atrocities, Jean-François ordered his execution. Toussaint wished there was another way, but his people were dying of starvation. Drastic steps were needed to curb the thirst for revenge and give the rebellion direction. Otherwise his people would go down.

So Jeannot, a black man, was executed by blacks for his atrocities against whites. No white had ever been executed for his crimes against the slaves. Despite their long years of ill treatment, the blacks were showing themselves more civilized than their masters.

The insurrection was now about three months old, and the blacks continued to fight in their reckless, frenzied way. Among the rebels were many who had no experience against cannons but who knew how to wage tribal warfare. As physician to the army, Toussaint often accompanied them out on forays.

A thousand blacks—men, women and children armed with machetes, rusty swords and other primitive weapons—would sweep down from a hill and advance on a white encampment. As they approached the enemy camp, the rebels set up such a howling and shrieking it sounded as if the doors to hell had suddenly opened. Then, when they were just beyond the range of the whites' guns, they became suddenly quiet.

For the whites in the camp the silence was far more nerve-racking than the noise. Watching carefully for the rebels to move within range of their guns, they could see a few blacks step forward and begin a demonic kind of dance, contorting their bodies into grotesque positions as voodoo priests chanted. The whites did not know what to expect next. Convinced they were surrounded, their hands sweating and their guns trembling, they waited, seemingly forever, for the attack to come.

It came with a terrible fury, as a thousand howling rebels rushed the camp, dodging bullets and cannon shot. The whites, greatly outnumbered, fired as fast as they could. Hundreds of blacks were shot down. Hundreds more kept coming. With knives drawn, they charged the whites' bayonets and flung themselves onto the horses, dragging the dragoons down from their mounts.

Such reckless courage tore at Toussaint's heart. Although the whites usually fled in panic, they left behind hundreds of blacks dead and dying. Rushing here and there, Toussaint bound wounds and did what he could to help the dying. But it was a hopeless task, and he felt helpless in the face of such a nightmare of death and blood.

After these forays the rebels returned to their camps, laden with guns, ammunition and food stolen from the whites. But their guerrilla tactics were effective only against isolated bands of whites. Against the heavily fortified cordons that confined them to the Northern Province, they were helpless. Unless the insurrection could spread out of the province, it was doomed to failure. Already hundreds of rebels had died of starvation. The rest were growing weaker and weaker. Then a rumor reached camp that an army was on its way from France to crush the revolt.

Jean-François and Biassou were scared. Toussaint was frightened too, but for his people, not for himself. He knew the rebels could not stand up against any massive attack. The two leaders came to Toussaint with a plan.

"We have decided," Jean-François informed Toussaint, "to make a peace offer to the commissioners. We want liberty for four hundred leaders, an additional free day a week for the slaves and a law prohibiting the use of the whip. In exchange we'll turn over all the rebels under our charge."

Toussaint stared at Jean-François in amazement. He knew that what the leaders were proposing was treachery. Unfortunately, the alternatives seemed no better. If he refused to go along with Biassou and Jean-François, they would carry out their plan without him. And if he warned the rebels to resist, he might just be leading them to their death. Without food and supplies, how long could they hold out? This way they would be slaves again, but at least they would be alive. And if the commissioners agreed to the terms, they would be better off than they had been before the uprising.

The two leaders were waiting for Toussaint's response. He felt ashamed for them as well as himself, but slowly he nodded his head in agreement. The next day he went to Le Cap with a group of rebels to present their offer.

The French commissioners were delighted with the proposal, but the planter-dominated Colonial Assembly was infuriated. "Bargain with criminals who have murdered our wives and burned our plantations? Give the rebel leaders their liberty? You must be mad!" responded the planters.

The commissioners protested, but the Assembly would not budge. "*All* the criminals must surrender unconditionally. They must return to their plantations immediately. If they don't, they will be hunted down and murdered to a man!"

Toussaint could not believe that he and the rebel leaders had humiliated and shamed themselves only to be flatly rejected. He saw to his dismay that the colonists who made up the Assembly were men blinded by pride, power, bigotry and a desire to punish the rebels. If the blacks returned to their plantations now, their fate would be worse than death. That day, Toussaint realized his people would never be safe until they were free.

The prospect of what lay ahead filled his soul with horror. He had not wanted violence. To save his people from further bloodshed, he had stooped to making compromises behind their backs. But the colonists, by their haughty rejection of the peace offer, had forced his hand. He would fight now, and he would not stop fighting until his people were free—all his people, not just the rebels. Having made this decision, Toussaint never wavered.

When he returned to camp, Toussaint angrily informed Jean-François and Biassou of all that had passed. "The commissioners are very well-meaning," he said, "but we cannot count on them for help. The Assembly, not the commissioners, holds the real power, and the Assembly has scorned our offer. We have no choice now but to fight with all the force we can muster."

The two leaders were amazed to hear the soft-spoken Toussaint speak so militantly. But the Colonial Assembly was not the only target of Toussaint's anger. He was fed up with Jean-François' and Biassou's type of leadership. He had stood on the sidelines long enough, watching them strut about as his people starved and hurled themselves over cannons. He informed the two leaders he was dropping his post as physician. "I'm going to train men for war," he said, and his tone silenced their objections.

Toussaint took the title of brigadier-general, and began the seemingly impossible task of turning half-naked, half-starved blacks into disciplined soldiers.

CHAPTER 4

JEAN-FRANÇOIS and Biassou liked the fripperies of military life, but not the hard work. They rarely gave their men any real military training. So confused were the rebels by the few cannons they had, they kept putting the powder in front of the cannonballs. When their primitive methods of attack succeeded, it was purely because of their raw courage and their superior numbers. Also, the French, accustomed to conventional battles in open fields, were often thrown into confusion by the guerrilla tactics. But Toussaint knew the blacks could never win major battles this way.

The rebels still had some white prisoners in their camp, among them a French officer who was indebted to Toussaint for rescuing him from a massacre. He agreed to help Toussaint train the blacks. Toussaint carefully hand-picked a hundred rebels he felt would make good, loyal fighting men, and, with the help of the French officer, began training them.

Toussaint was a patient but hard taskmaster. His men were hungry, weak and discouraged, but he subjected them to as rigid and exacting a routine as any well-fed French regiment. Insisting on strict obedience and respect, he tolerated no breach of discipline. Only the men's devotion to Toussaint kept them going.

The new brigadier-general quickly realized that neither his people nor Haiti's terrain was suited to classic military strategy, so he modified their training by mixing in the guerrilla tactics he had learned from his father—tactics his African-born soldiers were already familiar with. Soon his work showed such concrete results that a British officer who visited the camp was astounded. With open admiration he watched as the blacks, naked from the waist up and carrying only a sword, musket and ammunition bag, carried out their precision drills with a skill equal to anything he had seen in His Britannic Majesty's army.

While Jean-François and Biassou strutted, Toussaint worked. Soon he had several hundred men under his command. They were the elite of the rebel army. When Toussaint led them out on forays, there was no recklessness, no irresponsible loss of life. Now when the battles ended, instead of dead and dying blacks all over the field, there were dozens of white prisoners.

Toussaint's strategy surprised the French. Expecting the same primitive tactics employed by other rebels, they instead found themselves up against a new kind of adversary—a man with sound military knowledge who planned every move carefully and brilliantly. But Toussaint's army was very small, and despite their successes, they could not win the rebellion alone.

Haiti's Colonial Assembly continued to underplay the revolt. They did not want to risk any of their new power by admitting they couldn't handle the situation and asking France for assistance. The French commissioners, although very distressed by the slave uprising, were even more disturbed by colonists clamoring for independence. They were reluctant to further antagonize the colonists by criticizing the Assembly and insisting on French aid.

Smug and haughty, the Assembly contented itself with cordoning off the revolt and keeping the rebels in the Northern Province. They knew most of the rebels were starving. It was just a matter of time.

But discontent in Haiti was widespread now, too widespread to be held in check by a fortified cordon. The mulattoes in the Western Province, persecuted beyond their endurance by the Little Whites, rose up in revolt. Fighting broke out in Port-au-Prince, the chief city in the West, and mulatto men, women and children were massacred in the streets. A mulatto leader named Pinchinat sent out an eloquent call to battle, and the mulattoes responded in mass. The cry went up, "Long live liberty, long live equality, long live love!" Remembering why Ogé had failed, they put their own prejudices aside and called on the slaves in the West to join them.

The revolt in the West touched off a mulatto uprising in the South, and all three of Haiti's provinces were in revolt.

The situation in the West was what really alarmed the

whites. They knew the greatest threat to their power in the colony was an alliance between the mulattoes and the blacks. The Assembly, no longer so smug but still incapable of accepting any blame, hurled accusations at all the supporters of the French Revolution. France and its mulatto-loving revolutionaries were to blame for all the trouble in the colony. Not the colonists! Voices demanding independence from the mother country grew louder and more strident.

The French government was seriously alarmed. It could not afford to lose its richest colony. The wealthy French bourgeoisie with investments in Haiti—the same people who had proclaimed the Rights of Man and demanded liberty and equality—now saw their pockets threatened by the disorder in the colony. They demanded the restoration of "order" in Haiti.

One morning, about a year after the slave uprising had begun, there was considerable excitement in Toussaint's camp high on Morne Pélé. "A French army has landed! The soldiers are coming!"

Toussaint was not surprised. By now he had contacts in Paris who notified him of all that happened there. He knew an army of six thousand men was on its way from France.

From the moment it landed, the well-equipped French army began to make quick work of the ragged rebel forces. The first to suffer were the rebel bands who roamed the hills fighting under voodoo priests and African chieftains. Then the armies of Biassou and Jean-François were driven back into their mountain camps, where they began to fortify their position.

Toussaint now had five hundred men under his command. He continued to harass the French, making sudden, unexpected attacks on their camps at night and ambushing them as they marched through mountain passes. But his little army was no match for the French regiments, and Toussaint also was forced to retreat to the mountain stronghold, where he watched helplessly as famine and disease began to kill off his people. He did not stop those who wished to surrender. He knew how frail the hope of freedom he offered looked now. Soon, about fifteen thousand men, women and children had left the hills, begging the whites to take them back.

A combined army of French soldiers, Creoles and mulattoes prepared for the final assault.

Then, at the darkest moment for the rebels, reprieve came from an unexpected quarter. In France, events had moved ahead at a dizzy pace. Eager to spread the revolution throughout Europe and also avoid difficult internal problems, the government of France had declared war on Austria. In April of 1792 the French Revolutionary Wars began, and five months later France became a republic.

Royalty all over Europe was shocked. Right in their midst a new and terrifying monster had been born—a monster called "democracy." The execution of King Louis XVI and the revolutionary army's advance into Austria added to their alarm, and by March of 1793 Great Britain, Spain and Holland had joined the war against the new republic.

England and Spain had long envied France her rich little colony in the Caribbean, and Haiti now found herself threatened externally by two powerful countries—by Spain on her eastern border and by the English navy on her coasts.

The French army in Haiti had a new, more difficult task on its hands. To protect the colony from falling into Spanish and British hands, it needed all the strength it could muster. Reluctantly, the French army dropped its plans for a final assault against the rebels, and began to prepare for an invasion.

Toussaint could hardly believe his good fortune. One day he was trapped by the French, about to face almost certain defeat. The next day both the French and Spanish were making offers to the rebels, trying to seduce them over to their side.

Toussaint now had to decide where the best interests of his people lay—with the Spanish or the French. The Spanish offered money, arms, ammunition and a promise of freedom to any black who fought with them. The French offered little more than amnesty. Furthermore, Toussaint did not believe France could win the European war. How could the shaky new republic conquer the combined forces of Europe's most powerful armies? It made little sense to fight on the side of a country destined for defeat.

As Toussaint weighed the alternatives, a plan began to form in his mind. With the arms and supplies he got from the Spanish, he could build up his army so it would be a power to reckon with. Then he could bargain with the Spanish—his help in return for the emancipation of all Haiti's slaves. Toussaint was beginning to think like a politician.

Before making his decision, Toussaint decided to give the French one last chance. He wrote a letter to the commander-in-chief of the French army, General Laveaux, offering his help in return for liberty for all the slaves.

The Comte de Laveaux was an aristocrat who had fought bravely against the royalists in the French Revolution. A man of democratic leanings, he had sympathized with the blacks from the moment he landed in Haiti. But he was a soldier first, a man who carried out his country's orders. He did not dare grant liberty to the blacks, when he had been sent to restore "order." Laveaux refused Toussaint's offer, and the rebel leader headed across the border with six hundred men.

Many of the smaller rebel bands remained neutral, but Jean-François and Biassou, unable to resist the offers of money and military rank, had already joined the Spanish.

Toussaint was well received in the Spanish camp. He was by now not only the acknowledged political leader of the blacks, but the only rebel commander who had shown real military ability. He was also the only rebel leader whose mind was set on freedom for all the blacks, but this the Spanish did not know. They appointed Toussaint a Knight of the Order of Isabella, and he fought beside the Spanish under Spain's royalist flag. He was becoming very adept at the deceptive game circumstances forced him to play.

Many French royalist officers, disgusted with France's democratization and shocked by the execution of Louis XVI, had deserted the French army in Haiti and gone over to the Spanish. Figuring they could manipulate the "ignorant" ex-slaves easier than they could the Spaniards, they often chose to join the black forces. The royalist deserters who joined Toussaint's army were quickly disappointed. Toussaint put them to work drilling his troops, and they soon found themselves working so hard they had no time for intrigue.

Toussaint's army was now well fed and well equipped. With experienced officers to train and lead them, the blacks immediately began winning victories against the French.

In battle Toussaint was fearless, even reckless, charging at the head of his men, dodging bullets and cannonballs on all sides. The French, overcome by the speed and force of his attacks, often surrendered before realizing the enemy's small number.

Toussaint was wounded many times, but he never let this stop him. During one battle a spent cannonball hit him right in the face. His men, seeing him fall from his horse, rushed to his side, certain he was dead. Instead, Toussaint stood up, shook his head and remounted his horse. Smiling down at his astonished men, he displayed the cannonball's toll—several missing front teeth.

As a conqueror, Toussaint was honorable and humane. He never permitted his men to loot, make war on civil population or mistreat prisoners. Instead of being shot, prisoners were treated with courtesy. His reputation for discipline and humanity spread quickly. Many towns that would have resisted other rebel leaders to the bitter end often surrendered to Toussaint with token resistance. He became very successful at obtaining bloodless victories, employing such maneuvers as the one he used against the French Colonel Brandicourt.

One night Brandicourt, with a force of fifteen hundred men, was making his way through a mountain pass near Dondon in Haiti's Northern Province. Toussaint, with three hundred of his best men, was waiting to ambush him. As the French approached, the blacks hid behind trees and withheld their fire. Out of the silence of the night, Brandicourt suddenly heard a disembodied voice demand, "Who goes there?"

"France," replied Brandicourt.

At that moment a number of blacks who had positioned themselves strategically allowed their shadowy forms to become visible in the moonlight. Everywhere the French looked they seemed to see blacks—there must have been thousands!

"You are completely surrounded," the voice continued. "A battle can bring you no profit whatsoever. Let your commander come forth and speak to Toussaint Louverture. He will not be harmed."

Brandicourt immediately ordered his men to attack. But his men, convinced they were surrounded and outnumbered, begged him to confer with Toussaint. Having no choice, Brandicourt surrendered.

Without a shot being fired, the entire force went over to the blacks.

The next morning Toussaint headed into his camp. Behind him marched fifteen hundred French soldiers, drums beating and French flags flying. When the blacks in the camp saw this formidable force approaching, they beat a hasty retreat, certain the enemy was upon them.

Toussaint sped after them. "Wait, brothers, wait! These

are our allies now. They have surrendered. Toussaint would not lead the enemy into his own camp!"

With a wary eye on the French flags and uniforms, the blacks walked slowly back to camp. When they saw all the French guns and ammunition the rebels had captured, they forgot about their nervousness.

The Spanish soldiers were poorly trained for guerrilla warfare and unfamiliar with Haiti's rugged terrain. As Toussaint had planned, the government of Santo Domingo began to rely heavily on his little army. As soon as he felt his position was strong enough, Toussaint asked his Spanish commander, the Marquis d'Hermonas, to propose that Don García, the governor of Santo Domingo, offer freedom to all of Haiti's slaves. This would bring over to the Spanish side the nearly four hundred thousand slaves who had not rebelled, and Spain could then conquer Haiti with ease. The entire island would be Spanish, and the blacks would be Spanish citizens with equal rights under law.

After hearing the proposal from the Marquis, Don García stared in disbelief. "Free every slave in Haiti!" he roared. "Haven't I already given the promise of freedom to every black fighting at our side? Toussaint is a good man. But if he is not happy with our agreement, he can go over to the French."

After the Marquis left the room, the governor shook his head and muttered to himself, "Freedom for all the slaves. What a dreamer!"

When Toussaint learned of Don García's refusal, he thought to himself, I must be patient. Soon my army will be so strong I will not ask for liberty. I will demand it.

As Toussaint continued to strengthen his army and pile up victories against the French, the squabbles among the whites of Haiti approached the boiling point.

With the army it had sent to crush the slave revolt, the French government also sent a new commissioner named Sonthonax. His job was to restore order between the whites and mulattoes and to see that discrimination against the mulattoes was stopped. A staunch supporter of the ideals of the French Revolution, the fair-skinned, red-haired Sonthonax appointed mulattoes to the Colonial Assembly and threatened with severe penalties any white caught persecuting a mulatto. Then he made the whole colony gasp with disbelief. He appointed a black freedman to a government post.

Sonthonax quickly became the man most detested by the whites of Haiti. He had been in the colony several months when, in June of 1793, Galbaud, the new governor of Haiti, arrived.

The French government had selected Galbaud for the post because he was a military expert and the colony needed to build up its defenses. It was a foolish selection on the part of the French. Galbaud owned property in the colony, and naturally identified his interests with those of the planters. Haiti's planters were now, almost to a man, counterrevolutionaries, strongly opposed to the French Revolution and the democratic policies of the Republic.

The new governor lost no time in trying to undermine the power of the all-too-democratic Sonthonax. When Sonthonax got wind of what he was up to, he appealed to General Laveaux, the anti-royalist French commander. Galbaud was hustled aboard a warship bound for France.

But the admiral of the warship was a royalist, and Galbaud quickly won his support. More than one hundred French warships and merchant vessels were anchored in Le Cap's harbor. That night, under cover of darkness, Galbaud and the admiral lowered a boat into the water and rowed quietly from ship to ship, boarding each and arousing the crew.

"Sonthonax is a traitor," Galbaud hissed. "He supports the mulattoes over the whites. Are you going to let him hand our colony over to the mulattoes?"

Toussaint of Haiti

The sailors were supporters of the Revolution and the Rights of Man. But Galbaud succeeded in arousing their primitive instincts of racial fear and hatred. "Down with Sonthonax!" became their cry.

The next morning Galbaud returned to shore at the head of three thousand men. The Creoles of Le Cap, most of whom were counterrevolutionaries and all of whom hated Sonthonax, sided with Galbaud. Laveaux's troops were outnumbered, and Sonthonax and the other commissioners were forced to flee the city.

Sonthonax fled to the hills above Le Cap, and established his headquarters at Bréda. Ironically, the plantation that Toussaint had saved from destruction had become a strategic key to the defense of Le Cap against the black rebels. When darkness fell, one of Laveaux's officers arrived at the plantation house. "Galbaud is gaining," he warned. "Our troops can't hold him. They want to surrender."

Sonthonax did not reply. Instead, he left the room and walked out onto the veranda. Yes, the fires he had seen earlier were still burning in the distance. He knew that two bands of black rebels who had remained neutral were camped in the hills. After staring thoughtfully at the fires, he turned abruptly and walked back into the house.

Addressing the other commissioners, Sonthonax said, "Galbaud and his planter friends must not take Le Cap. We have no choice. We must ask the blacks for help."

Turning to the French officer, Sonthonax said, "Ride to the rebel camp. Tell them we promise freedom to all blacks who will fight with us against Galbaud. They will be the equals of whites, with all the rights and privileges of a French citizen."

The astonished officer galloped off toward the fires in the hills, a white flag in his hand.

That night the sounds of hilarity rang through Le Cap.

Laveaux had retreated and Galbaud's sailors were happily looting the city's shops and warehouses, getting drunk on the rum they stole. The cafés were filled with boisterous, victorious sailors holding giggling Creole women in their arms.

At first they mistook the distant roar for thunder. As the roar grew louder, the sailors stopped their celebrating to listen. A minute later they dropped their loot, their rum and their women and ran for their lives.

Fifteen thousand rebels swooped down from the hills and swarmed through the streets of the city, routing the sailors from the shops and cafés, forcing them back to the harbor. There the terrified sailors leaped into their boats and rowed rapidly out to their ships, away from the demonic-seeming hordes that pursued them. The blacks had accepted Sonthonax's offer.

In the course of the battle, fire broke out and quickly spread through the city. Thousands of Creoles, carrying whatever possessions they could save, rushed through the burning streets to the harbor, where they too climbed into boats and rowed out to the ships. In their haste they overcrowded the boats, and many turned over, drowning scores of men, women and children.

The one hundred ships in Le Cap's harbor pulled up anchor and set sail for the United States. They carried with them ten thousand refugees, mostly Creole counterrevolutionaries, who settled in coastal states such as New York, Massachusetts and Virginia. They left behind a city in charred ruins, strewn with the corpses of blacks, whites and mulattoes.

Sonthonax returned to the "Paris of the Antilles" to find two thirds of it burned to the ground.

The black rebels, unlike the French sailors, had not stayed around to loot or celebrate. As suddenly as they had appeared, they disappeared, returning to their camps in the hills. But they returned to their camps as free men, their liberty guaranteed by Sonthonax. The slaves of Le Cap, learning their brothers in the hills had been given freedom, began marching through the streets, shouting their demands for liberty. Mothers, wives, sisters and sweethearts of the freed rebels claimed they too had a right to be free since their men had fought for Sonthonax. The city was truly out of hand.

Sonthonax was in an extremely bad position. Toussaint had already captured many fortified posts for the Spanish in the Northern Province. The size of Laveaux's army had been greatly reduced by the battle with Galbaud, and by the time reinforcements arrived, it might be too late—for Sonthonax knew a British invasion was imminent.

The commissioner had no choice but to turn to the blacks again for help. In August of 1793 he took the decisive step. He declared the abolition of slavery in Haiti. He pleaded with all blacks to rally to the cause of the French Republic.

As the news spread through Le Cap, the blacks rushed through the streets weeping, shouting, dancing and singing. Huge crowds of freed slaves gathered in front of Sonthonax's home shouting, "Long live Sonthonax!"

Deeply moved, the commissioner stepped out onto his balcony and spoke to them as no white man had before. "I promise that until my dying day I will support the rights of mulattoes, Africans and descendants of Africans."

No longer slaves, but free people, the blacks cheered wildly. All night long they celebrated. The Creoles slunk into their homes and closed their shutters, their hearts heavy with bitterness and resentment. But they consoled each other with the assurances that the French government would soon put Sonthonax and the blacks in their place. France could not afford to free the slaves.

The departure of ten thousand Creoles, together with Sonthonax's abolition of slavery, marked the beginning of the end of white domination in Haiti. The whites, quarreling among themselves, had laid the groundwork for their own downfall and for the rise of Toussaint Louverture and the blacks.

CHAPTER 5

NEWS of Sonthonax's proclamation swept through the colony. When it reached Toussaint's camp, his men began whooping and shouting for joy, but Toussaint knew their celebration was premature. The haughty planters would almost certainly ignore the proclamation. Until the French government declared it official, Toussaint would stay where he was. He was learning to be cautious in his dealings with the French.

Toussaint was staying with the Spanish, but to see all his people free—to see them citizens of Haiti with equal rights—was now the consuming goal of his life. To achieve this he knew he had to reach beyond the rebels, to rally all the blacks around the cause. Toussaint made his first plea for unity, and his aides read it to blacks throughout the colony.

"Brothers and Friends. The name of Toussaint Louverture is perhaps known to you. I have taken it on myself to avenge my people. I need your help. Wherever you are, unite yourselves and fight for the cause. Those who can, come join me and fight by my side. I will not rest until liberty and equality reign throughout Haiti!"

Jean-François and Biassou, having no interest in liberty for their people, remained with the Spanish, but more and more of their men began joining Toussaint's forces.

With his rapidly growing army, Toussaint struck blow after blow at the French. He took, in rapid succession, Gros-

Morne, Marmelade, Plaisance, Limbé and several other towns. Soon, thanks to Toussaint's victories, the Spanish held every fortified post in Haiti's Northern Province except Le Cap and two other towns.

Toussaint's military genius was being grudgingly acknowledged even by his enemies. Unlike Jean-François and Biassou, he did not work at inspiring awe in his men. He wore only a simple field uniform, with the familiar madras handkerchief on his head, and lived and fought side by side with his soldiers, eating the same rations and sharing all their dangers and hardships. If he saw an artillery man struggling to move a cannon, he did not order a soldier to assist the man. He himself dismounted and helped with the cannon, once nearly crushing his hand in the process.

As Toussaint suspected, many of the planters in Haiti ignored Sonthonax's proclamation. Most of the blacks who had not joined the slave revolt were still slaves. Whenever Toussaint conquered a town, his first act was to free the slaves. Even in the Spanish colony, where no one had declared slavery abolished, Toussaint continued to rally the blacks to freedom right under the Spaniard's royalist noses. Each day his hold on the masses grew stronger. Jean-François and Biassou became jealous of his power, and the Spaniards wondered and grew a little nervous.

Biassou's resentment reached such a peak he went to see the Spanish governor, Don García. "Toussaint is a traitor. He's not fighting for you. He's fighting for himself. Everywhere he goes he arms the slaves and tells them they're free. We demand the head of this guilty man!"

Don García was not about to execute such a valuable man as Toussaint. But he promised Biassou steps would be taken to check Toussaint's power and stop him from freeing more slaves.

Meanwhile, Toussaint was growing increasingly uneasy in

the service of Spain. It was clear the Spanish meant to uphold slavery at all costs, and if they would not free their own slaves, how could the rebels be sure of their future freedom? To make matters worse, Spain was in alliance with England, and an English fleet was on its way to Haiti. Toussaint knew that whenever the British occupied a territory, they restored slavery.

The Creoles knew this too. They actually welcomed the prospect of a British invasion.

When it came, in September of 1793, the British "invaders" found themselves warmly greeted, even embraced, by noisy Creoles waving British flags. Nowhere in Jérémie, the coastal town in southern Haiti where they landed, did the British see a single French flag. For most of the Creoles, the last vestige of loyalty to France had been shattered when Sonthonax abolished slavery.

With such a welcome, the British made swift advances against the French. Many French royalist officers surrendered without a fight, and one coastal town after another fell. By early 1794 the invaders held the whole Western Province and most of the South. In the North, Toussaint was in control.

General Laveaux, the French commander, was a loyal and courageous soldier, but he was at his wit's end. Entrenched in Port-de-Paix in northern Haiti with the remnants of his weary, ill-equipped army, he was hemmed in on all sides—by the British, the Spanish *and* Toussaint. France, having taken on much of Europe, had no soldiers or supplies to spare.

The beleaguered Laveaux sent a desperate message to Sonthonax at Le Cap, which was still in French hands.

"Our misery is truly great. For six months bread and rations were reduced to six ounces a day for officers and men. Now all the bread is gone. My men have no shoes or shirts. They are fighting barefoot like the Africans. We are almost out of ammunition."

Toussaint of Haiti

Toussaint's fortunes were on the rise, and the army of the French Republic was half-naked, barefoot and hungry.

British-Spanish conquest of the world's richest colony was only days away. It was a precarious moment in history. If France lost Haiti, Spain and England would use the colony's enormous wealth to help crush the army of the French Republic in Europe, and England would once again be a power in American waters. For the United States, Haiti's neighbor to the north, the memory of British oppression was still fresh. The weak young country followed events in Haiti with concern, dreading the prospect of a powerful British base in the Caribbean.

Toussaint, too, was troubled. He knew that by fighting with the Spanish he was helping the British gain control of Haiti. He was still uncertain about the blacks' future under Spain, but he had no doubts what a future under the British held. As he brooded over the complex political situation, events in France once again brought him to a decision that would change the course of events in Haiti.

France was still in ferment, caught up in the frenzy of revolutionary zeal. "Down with tyranny! Down with oppression!" the servants, peasants and laborers had cried. Now they added a new demand: "Down with slavery!"

It was easy for the bourgeois gentleman sitting in the France's National Convention to forget the slaves. But the people, knew what slavery meant. They felt a bond with all oppressed people, and now that they had power, they did not forget the slaves. The masses of France stopped drinking coffee. "This is not coffee that fills our cups! It is the blood of our black brothers in Haiti!"

Nothing would still their voices. The National Convention, alarmed by their revolutionary ardor, was forced to listen. When Sonthonax sent three deputies—one white, one mulatto and one black—to seek representation and appeal for passage of his proclamation, the Convention was forced to accept them.

As the black and mulatto deputies entered the assembly hall, the entire all-white Convention rose to their feet and applauded. Those planters and merchants who imagined their fortunes going out the back door as the deputies entered the front door also rose. They did not dare do otherwise. The tide of revolutionary ferment was too strong.

The black deputy made a brief but impassioned speech, outlining the horrors of slavery and appealing for acceptance of Sonthonax's proclamation. He promised that all the blacks of Haiti would throw their support behind the beleagured French forces in the colony.

After he sat down, a member of the Convention arose and addressed the President. "When we drew up the constitution of the French people, we forgot the unhappy slaves. History will reproach us for that. We must repair this wrong. Mr. President, let us not dishonor ourselves further by even discussing the matter. Let us proclaim liberty for all the blacks this very moment!"

Revolutionary France was at last becoming true to its proclaimed ideals of liberty and equality. On this historic day in February of 1794, the French Republic confirmed Sonthonax's emancipation proclamation and abolished slavery in *all* its colonies. No longer could the slaveowners ignore the proclamation.

It was sometime in April that the brooding Toussaint learned the news. He did not hesitate. Now he and France were fighting for the same thing.

General Laveaux, only days away from total defeat, received a simple message from Toussaint offering his aid. The French commander sent a speedy reply to Toussaint expressing his appreciation and appointing Toussaint commander of the Cordon of the West. The black general then called his officers together.

"Brothers, Toussaint has been deceived by the enemies of the Republic. But what man can honestly claim he has escaped every pitfall? The Spanish have not freed their slaves. The British will surely restore slavery if they get control. Only the French Republic has declared the slaves free. I have offered my services to the commander-in-chief of the revolutionary French forces, and he has graciously accepted. Will you join me, brothers?"

The response was unanimous. "We acknowledge no leader other than Toussaint Louverture. Our men will follow wherever you go."

Toussaint expressed his gratitude and then warned his officers: "We must act with supreme caution. We're surrounded on all sides by the Spanish and forces friendly to them. Until we make our first move, go about your duties in a normal way. Avoid arousing suspicion at all costs."

Before making a move against the Spanish, Toussaint secretly arranged for his family to be driven back over the border to a plantation in Haiti's Northern Province. Then he was ready.

The first maneuver Toussaint planned was distasteful to him. Biassou and Jean-François were now the darlings of the Creole planters. Often they moved into a town where Toussaint had freed the slaves and forced their black brothers back to the plantations and slavery. They were traitors to their own people and the cause of liberty. Still Toussaint did not relish turning on his former chiefs. He had no alternative. While his brother Paul, now one of his most trusted and capable officers, kept Jean-François in check, Toussaint and a band of hand-picked men fell on Biassou's camp, scattering the startled rebels in all directions.

Toussaint then hastened to his brother's aid, and Jean-François met the same fate as his accomplice, Biassou. Reporting to Laveaux on the hasty departure of his former chief, Toussaint said wryly, "Jean-François owes his escape to the thickness of the underbrush into which he fled. I am in possession of his shirt and breeches, which he left behind. My men have taken many prisoners."

Biassou and Jean-François survived Toussaint's surprise attack, but they were demoralized, and never regained their former power. Many more of the rebels serving under them went over to Toussaint, increasing his army to five thousand men.

The black commander now turned his attention to the Spanish and the complacent, unsuspecting British. Weaving rapidly in and out of Haiti's rugged hills, he scattered now a British force, now a Spanish force, now a British force. The Spanish, thrown into confusion by Toussaint's desertion, put up a poor fight, and soon he had recaptured for the French all the fortified posts he had won for the Spanish.

The swiftness of Toussaint's movements and his guerrilla tactics baffled the British. A harried British officer reported to his commander, "Toussaint appears, then he disappears—as if by magic. Then he reappears where we least expect him. He seems to be everywhere! Where does his army camp? What do his men live on? Where do they get their supplies? We have tried and tried to get this information, but still we don't know. Toussaint, on the other hand, is all too well informed about everything that goes on in our camp."

The speed with which Toussaint's army moved was one of its major tactical advantages. Familiar with the terrain, the blacks could move swiftly even along trails so overgrown they had to hack their way through. And they traveled light, carrying only small arms and a little heavy artillery. The ponderous Spanish and British troops, loaded down with supplies and ammunition, couldn't begin to keep up with them.

Unlike the white soldiers, who were accustomed to an easier way of life, the former slaves were inured to physical hardship. They marched barefoot over the hot, rough, often bristly ground, under a relentless sun, for hours without resting. They had little to eat, but hunger was hardly a new sensation for them. And they were fighting for their freedom—not working to make their detested masters rich.

Toussaint reported to Laveaux, "My men have no coats, shirts, trousers or shoes. The rags they wear cover only a small part of their bodies. But they are fighting for freedom, and their morale is high."

Their appearance was ragged, and the equipment shabby. Yet they were a formidable little army. Their courage was so great, their determination so fierce, that even when the ammunition gave out in battle they kept on fighting. They loaded their guns with stones, drew their knives and, dodging musket and cannon shot, put up such a savage battle the enemy finally withdrew, exhausted and amazed. Toussaint's own bravery in battle was such that his men, forgetting all personal risk, followed him without hesitation.

But Toussaint was frustrated by a shortage of heavy artillery. Without it he could not recapture the heavily fortified coastal towns, because of the big guns of the British warships in the harbors. For the time being he had to concentrate on the enemy's interior positions, which were more vulnerable to the bush tactics in which his men excelled.

Toussaint invaded Haiti's Western Province. After several months of hard fighting, he defeated a large Spanish force under the Marquis d' Espinville on the plains near the town of Mirebalais. The Spanish were forced to retreat to the fortified town, but the blacks pursued and surrounded them. As their supplies ran out, the Spaniards' situation grew increasingly desperate. The Marquis finally requested an interview with Toussaint.

"I give you my promise that if you surrender, no one will be shot," Toussaint told him. "More than that, if any of your men wish to join my army, they may do so."

As usual, Toussaint kept his word, and many of the prisoners joined his army. The town of Mirebalais, with its pleasant waterfalls, gardens, and orchards, so appealed to the black commander he set up headquarters there.

Toussaint's bloodless victories and his courteous treatment of prisoners continued to enhance his reputation as a humane and disciplined soldier. The whites of Haiti were beginning to feel they could trust this man, even if he was a rebel and an ex-slave. By contrast, they despised and feared Jean-François and Biassou, who continued to wreak their revenge on the French.

One Sunday morning, hundreds of French people were worshipping peacefully in a Roman Catholic church in Port-au-Prince. When the service ended and the men, women and children began to leave, Jean-François' soldiers burst into the church and slaughtered every one of the innocent worshippers.

When he heard of the massacre, Toussaint trembled with rage. "I have always had a horror of men who get satisfaction out of shedding blood," he commented to Laveaux. "As for Toussaint, General, you may rely on his feelings of humanity."

Toussaint had been fighting to restore French rule in Haiti for about a year when an unexpected event occurred. In the summer of 1795, Spain signed a peace treaty with France, and the entire Spanish colony of Santo Domingo was ceded to the French. The Spanish troops were to remain until a French garrison arrived, but the French feared Biassou and Jean-

François so much their armies were immediately disbanded. Many whites, remembering the massacre in the church, clamored for their heads, but Toussaint persuaded the French to allow his former chiefs to leave the country alive.

With the departure of Jean-François and Biassou from Haiti, Toussaint, the man they had deigned to make physician to their army, became the undisputed leader of Haiti's blacks. Most of the remaining rebels who had served under the two chiefs joined Toussaint's army. Although he carefully informed General Laveaux of his every move, the black leader was now in virtually unchecked command of his army.

The Spanish out of the way, Toussaint turned his full attention on the British—the formidable colonial monster that would devour his people. France, paralyzed by her European involvements, rested all her hopes on Toussaint. Whether Haiti remained French or fell under British rule now lay in the hands of the former slave and his loyal army of blacks.

CHAPTER 6

SPAIN's surrender, far from discouraging the British, only heightened their desire for victory. Now if they defeated the French, Haiti would be *all* theirs. Immediately the British government began pouring more men and supplies into the war-torn little colony.

Toussaint was waging a brilliant campaign against the British, but his victories were never decisive. He needed heavy artillery and more men. And his troops and his people needed food. When he was not busy fighting the British, Toussaint worked to restore agriculture. He tried to persuade blacks who did not join his army to remain on their plantations, as paid cultivators or laborers. He invited the planters who had fled to return and recultivate their burned plantations, and persuaded those who had not left to remain. He even told the royalist planters who had deserted and gone over to the Spanish that they could return if they took a vow of allegiance to the French Republic.

Toussaint's lenient attitude toward the royalist planters brought grumblings from all sides—from the black laborers, his officers and the French Commissioner Sonthonax. Toussaint had no love for the traitorous planters either, but he was determined to restore agriculture. "Only in agricultural prosperity can the freedom of the blacks be assured!" he warned Sonthonax.

To the laborers, Toussaint said, "Victory against the British is impossible without food and supplies. We need crops to eat and to export. From the exports will come revenue to buy weapons and ammunition. If you desert your plantations, who will till the soil, who will harvest the crops?"

Working on the plantations, even as paid laborers, was not the blacks' idea of freedom. Because they feared and respected Toussaint, they obeyed. But there was much discontent, and the British managed to stir up many an insurrection against the French.

Once the British had the blacks and French busy killing each other, they moved in, took over the town—and restored slavery.

"It is always the blacks who suffer the most!" Toussaint would cry on hearing such news. "Will my people always be the plaything of these monsters whom hell has loosed upon the colony?"

Toussaint worked hard to win his people's trust, and before long the British found their trouble-making thwarted.

The whites too were beginning to cooperate with the black general whose troops displayed such discipline.

When Toussaint's soldiers entered a town, many whites, terrified at first by the sight of thousands of half-naked blacks armed with guns and knives, barricaded themselves in their homes. They waited, trembling in fear, for the blacks to break down their doors, rob their homes and steal their women. Considering how they had treated the slaves, they had little right to expect anything better. But as the day progressed and no such horrors occurred, the nervous whites ventured timidly out into the streets. There, to their astonishment, they found the armed blacks patrolling the town and the townspeople going about their business unmolested. If they approached one of the soldiers, he either ignored them or treated them with cool politeness.

Many of Toussaint's soldiers had been brutally treated as slaves. Now that they were armed and the whites defenseless, they found restraining their desire for revenge exceedingly difficult. That they obeyed was a vivid testimony to their self-restraint and the effectiveness of Toussaint's teaching.

"Do not imitate your former masters by indulging in acts of cruelty," he would lecture his soldiers. "Vengeance is demoralizing and self-injurious. It is not possible to wreak vengeance without injuring yourselves and your brothers. Show yourselves worthy of liberty. Be superior to those who would chain you and call you savage and wild."

The planters, impressed with Toussaint's humane attitude toward the whites and the hold he had over his soldiers, did not flee, even when the blacks occupied their district. Many of those who had fled, learning Toussaint could be trusted, returned and recultivated their plantations.

Toussaint was winning the love and trust of the blacks and

at least the cooperation of the whites. But the proud, haughty mulattoes were a problem.

The revolutionary government of France had given mulattoes their rights, and most of them were fiercely loyal to the Republic. Fearing all royalists, they waged a valiant struggle against the British in every province. Toussaint's cooperation with the royalist planters angered them, and many mulattoes regarded him as a traitor to the Republic. Above all, they feared his power. They feared Haiti would be dominated by blacks when they, the mulattoes, were so obviously the natural heirs to power.

The leading mulatto in Haiti was André Rigaud, the bold, adventurous son of a French nobleman and a Haitian black woman. Handsome and dark-skinned, small in stature, Rigaud had been educated in Paris, where he acquired a very polished manner. Like many of Haiti's mulattoes, he had fought with the French in the American Revolution. His mulatto army was courageous and well trained, and as a general Rigaud ranked second in importance only to Toussaint.

Rigaud was a determined soldier, and in the South his army gave the British no rest. He was also vain and proud, and chafed at being second to a black. It was his dream to see the mulattoes the ruling class of Haiti and himself the most powerful man in the colony. Two men stood in the way of his dream —Toussaint, the leading black, and General Laveaux, the commander-in-chief of the French forces and now also governor of Haiti.

In his daily contact with the blacks of Haiti, the aristocratic General Laveaux had come to love them. He had no use for whites or mulattoes who refused to treat his black friends as equals. And of all the men in the colony, the one he felt the deepest affection and greatest admiration for was Toussaint Louverture.

Toussaint was by nature reserved, and had never been intimate with any man. As a black man in power, he had many enemies and was forced to be somewhat wary of everyone around him. Laveaux was a white man and Toussaint's former enemy. But he was a man so gentle and good, whose high esteem for Toussaint was so obviously sincere, that he melted the black leader's reserve and the two men became close friends. Their friendship created a strong alliance of power between the French and the blacks—a bond that frustrated Rigaud and the mulattoes.

If Rigaud were to rule Haiti, one of the two men had to be removed. Toussaint was too well protected by his army, which was much larger than Rigaud's. Laveaux, however, now concentrated on administrative duties, leaving all military affairs to Toussaint, and hence he no longer had a regular army of his own.

Laveaux's headquarters were in the government palace of Le Cap, and military command of the city itself was in the hands of a mulatto general named Villate. A vain, ambitious man, Villate was only too willing to help Rigaud get rid of Laveaux. Of course, they could not make a move without the cooperation of the city's blacks.

Whispers started all over Le Cap.

"General Laveaux has sold out to the British! They have given him five thousand francs."

"Laveaux has filled a whole warehouse down by the quay with chains!"

"A British fleet is outside the harbor, waiting for Laveaux's signal!"

The majority of Le Cap's blacks, so accustomed to white treachery, believed the rumors.

Laveaux was no fool. In his report to the French Minister of Marine, he said, "So great is Rigaud's pride and ambition that he dreams of becoming dictator of Haiti! If it weren't for the blacks, who support liberty and the Republic, I strongly believe the mulattoes would have already moved to control the colony."

After breakfast one morning, Laveaux sat down at his writing table to compose a letter to Toussaint. "Because of my love for my country I have endured the threats of the mulattoes with patience," he began.

He got no further. The doors on both ends of the drawing room were flung open, and a hundred mulattoes burst in. Laveaux, despite his suspicions, never dreamed the mulattoes would try to arrest him. Thinking they had come to have him settle a quarrel, he rose calmly from his desk. "What can I do for you, citizens?" he asked.

Shouting and cursing in reply, the mulattoes threw themselves on Laveaux and pummeled him with their fists. The elderly commander was putting up a stout struggle when Villate entered the room. "General, you're under arrest. The people no longer have confidence in you. They are begging me to replace you. Reluctantly, out of a sense of duty, I have accepted."

Laveaux was dragged out of the palace and thrown into prison like a common thief. Mulatto soldiers now patrolled the streets of Le Cap. Any black who resisted the coup was thrown into prison. The mulattoes were jubilant. Their bid for power had succeeded!

Outside Le Cap, Pierre Michel, a black colonel, was camped with four thousand men. When he learned of the coup, he immediately sent a dispatch rider to Toussaint, then encamped at Gonaïves, about seventy miles away.

"What! They have dared to arrest General Laveaux!" Toussaint cried on hearing the news. "What has got into them? Do they think they can do as they please? If I have to, I'll die a thousand deaths to bring them to their senses!"

Toussaint then summoned his leading generals—his brother Paul, his nephew Moyse and two blacks who were to play a major role in Haiti's history, Henri Christophe and Jean Jacques Dessalines.

To Dessalines, Toussaint said, "Take six thousand men and rendezvous with Colonel Michel outside Le Cap. With ten thousand men massed on the outskirts of the city, we'll make such a show of power Villate won't dare resort to arms. Civil war must be avoided!"

Then to Christophe, "Arouse the laborers on the plantations outside Le Cap. Order them to enter the city demanding Laveaux's release. But direct them to harm no one!"

Toussaint himself remained at Gonaïves. He sent an angry letter to Villate demanding Laveaux's release and a proclamation to the mulattoes and blacks of Le Cap:

"In showing contempt for General Laveaux, you have shown contempt for the Republic of France. Perhaps you would prefer to live under the English flag. If that is your desire I suggest you cast a glance at the district of Limbé. There the English, who call themselves 'liberators,' have chained your brothers and turned them into galley slaves. The women of color have been forced to flee their homes and hide in the woods to escape their barbarity. You, on the other hand, have been given freedom and equality. You *could* live peaceably and without fear. But no, you must sow confusion!"

Toussaint's orders were carried out swiftly and effectively. While ten thousand blacks waited outside the city, thousands of black laborers entered Le Cap and marched through the streets shouting, "Free General Laveaux! Laveaux is our friend! Free Laveaux!"

Faced with such massive opposition, the frightened Villate fled the city. Laveaux was freed, and the citizens of Le Cap again swore loyalty to Laveaux and the Republic.

On April 1, 1796, a triumphant Toussaint, surrounded by his elite bodyguard, entered Le Cap at the head of ten thousand troops of infantry, cavalry and artillery. Thousands of whites, grateful to Toussaint for restoring order to the city, lined the streets waving French flags and cheering as loudly as the blacks. Acknowledging their cheers with a modest nod, the black general, a proud, erect figure on a white stallion, rode slowly through the crowded streets—the same streets along which a quiet, obedient slave had driven his master not so long ago.

In the Place d'Armes, General Laveaux waited to greet his friend and deliverer. When Toussaint saw the French commander, still pale and shaken from his experience, he dismounted and rushed toward him. As the two men embraced, the band played the *Marseillaise*, and the people cheered wildly.

Laveaux stepped up to a speaker's stand and called for silence. The music stopped. Making no attempt to conceal the strong emotions he felt, Laveaux pointed to Toussaint and said, "There, my friends, stands Haiti's Spartacus! There stands the black who the philosopher Raynal predicted would one day appear and raise the standard of liberty. Toussaint Louverture is that courageous chief whose destiny it is to avenge the outrages committed against his race!"

Moved by such a eulogy, Toussaint raised his sword and cried, "After God—Laveaux!"

Laveaux smiled gently at this spontaneous outburst from so reserved a man as Toussaint. But beneath his smile he was tired and sad. He knew, and he knew Toussaint knew, he could no longer control the colony. The mulatto coup had shown not only that the mulattoes wanted to remove him but that the blacks did not really trust him because he was white. There was only one man in Haiti whom the blacks could be trusted to obey, only one man with enough influence and power to keep peace in the explosive little colony.

So, ending his speech, Laveaux said, "And I hereby appoint Toussaint Louverture, commander of the Cordon of the West, as my first assistant and lieutenant governor of the colony. Furthermore, I promise all of you I will take no action in any matter regarding the colony without first consulting with my dear friend and assistant, the lieutenant governor of Haiti!"

The blacks could not control their joy. The entire square resounded with their approving shouts. Now, when the government spoke, it would be Toussaint speaking—their voice, the voice of the people, a voice they could trust. Even many of the whites were pleased, for they had been forced to recognize that only Toussaint could keep the colony from being torn apart internally by various warring factions.

The mulattoes were stunned. They had felt confident Laveaux would appoint a mulatto as his assistant to prevent further trouble in Le Cap. Instead, he appointed a black, a former slave, a "friend" of the royalists, a "traitor" to the Republic. It was a great blow to their pride to be governed by an "inferior."

Toussaint was hurt and angered by the bitterness of the mulattoes, whom he considered brothers of the blood. He laid the entire blame for the attempted coup on Rigaud and accused the mulatto of disliking to serve under him because he was black.

Rigaud denied his role in the coup and Toussaint, knowing that only the British would benefit from their squabbling, forgave Rigaud and did all he could to minimize their differences.

Laveaux continued to hold his title, but henceforth he was

governor and commander-in-chief in name only. The true reins of power lay in the hands of Toussaint Louverture. It was only his iron will that kept Haiti pieced together. It was only his army that stood between Haiti and that persistent, insatiable devourer, the British Empire.

CHAPTER 7

RIGAUD and Toussaint, working together, pushed the British out of Haiti's interior. By the end of 1796 the invaders controlled only a long, narrow strip of strategic towns along the west coast of Haiti. While Rigaud held the British from advancing back into the interior in the South, Toussaint gave them no rest in the North. Threading unobserved through the valleys at night, his army would fall on a British post somewhere along the coast, inflict serious damage and disappear before reinforcements could be brought in from a neighboring position.

British soldiers were dying by the thousands. Those who did not fall in battle were struck down by yellow fever, a dreaded tropical disease to which the blacks and most Creoles were immune. Still reinforcements and money poured in. The British Empire seemed to have an endless supply of young men to throw away on its newest colonial venture. Their army in Haiti now consisted of twenty thousand well-trained, well-equipped veteran soldiers. Toussaint had only sixteen thousand well-trained but ragged and ill-equipped men.

For another whole year Toussaint harassed the British unrelentingly. Still he could not dislodge them from the coastal towns where the big guns of the famous English navy loomed protectively in the harbors. He *had* to have heavy artillery. Again Laveaux pleaded with France.

The French Republic, still embroiled in her European war, could not spare a man for the colony fighting so hard to stay French. When she finally managed to send some supplies, including heavy artillery, the British blockade prevented the French ship from reaching Haiti's shores.

There would be no heavy artillery for Toussaint's army. The black general realized he had to change his strategy.

Calling together his generals, Toussaint advised them, "We will fight a delaying action until the rainy season comes. When the rains come, yellow fever will cripple the British. Then we will launch a final, decisive campaign to rid Haiti of the royalist plague. France, England, the whole world will see what our black army can do!"

The generals were delighted. This must mean that heavy artillery was on its way. When they asked Toussaint where it was coming from, he replied, "There is no heavy artillery."

"No heavy artillery!" shouted General Moyse, leaping to his feet. "The British have cannons and warships. We can't fight cannons and warships with half-naked men and muskets!"

"For liberty, men will fight with bare hands," said Toussaint calmly. "It is not what you fight with that is important. It is what you're fighting for."

No one believed Toussaint could do it—except Toussaint, and he never wavered in his conviction.

In February of 1798, Toussaint ordered the assault on the British lines. The night before the attack he addressed all his men, holding a letter which he shook in the air.

"In my hand is a letter I have written to General Maitland, head of the British forces, protesting the barbarous behavior of his troops toward prisoners and citizens of occupied towns. Brothers, the enemy engages in looting and shooting prisoners to their heart's content. But you are not the British. You are men of honor. Tomorrow you go to rout the royalist oppressors, not to loot and kill. It is liberty, the most priceless possession on earth, not common booty we're fighting for. Do not disappoint me. Show that you're men who value liberty and know how to preserve it—for yourselves, your families and all your brothers!"

Toussaint and his officers then went into a huddle over a crude little map which the black leader himself had drawn up. When Toussaint was not completely familiar with an area, he would call in people who were and barrage them with questions. By asking where is this and how far is it from that and by applying his basic knowledge of geometry, he was able to draw up reasonably accurate maps of battle areas.

"Let's go over our strategy once again," he said to his generals. Running his finger along the map, he continued, "The British are strung out in a long thin line along the coast from Môle St.-Nicholas, here in the North, to Jérémie, here in the South. Rigaud will march into Grande Anse with eight thousand men and take Jérémie. At the same time the mulatto army under Beauvais will attack the British camps protecting Port-au-Prince in the West. We will drive the British out of the Artibonite Valley and the northwest."

Toussaint stopped and looked at his generals. In the flickering candlelight their faces looked tense and determined. Toussaint's courage and confidence had been contagious. They still had their doubts, but nothing short of death would stop them now.

"We'll make a massive attack against only one part of the line at a time in our section," Toussaint continued. "This will give us a numerical advantage we wouldn't have otherwise. Without heavy artillery we'll have to overwhelm them with numbers. Of course, it will also expose us to a flanking movement if the British decide to attempt it. We hope they will not. If they do, we'll have to rely on our mobility to cut them from their base."

When British spies discovered Toussaint was planning a massive offensive, they of course immediately informed General Maitland. The head of the British forces was not concerned. "Toussaint is an able guerrilla leader," Maitland conceded, "but he is not capable of any major military operation."

Maitland paid dearly for this underestimation of Toussaint. When the black general launched his "blitz," the British were caught completely off guard. In seven days Toussaint won seven victories. Soon he had back most of the fortified line. Too late the British realized they were dealing with a man who was not only an able guerrilla leader but a brilliant military tactician as well.

The army of His Britannic Majesty was teetering on the brink of disaster. As Toussaint had anticipated, the scourge of yellow fever returned with the rainy season, and the enemy's camp hospitals overflowed with the sick and wounded. Maitland finally requested permission to evacuate several towns. Toussaint knew he could press on and crush the British posts. He preferred, however, to save lives rather than adorn himself with more glory. Without incident, the British were allowed to move out of Port-au-Prince and several other towns.

On a beautiful day in April of 1798, Toussaint made his entry into Port-au-Prince. A long procession greeted him on the outskirts of the city and escorted him into the provincial capital. Two acolytes carrying a cross and banner headed the procession. Behind them came choirboys burning incense, members of the clergy, beautiful Creole ladies in open carriages and a guard of honor made up of young Creole men, mostly sons of wealthy planters. And behind Toussaint—his proud army.

Triumphal arches covered with roses, Toussaint's favorite flower, were set up along the street, and everywhere French flags flapped in the breeze. Crowds of whites, mulattoes and blacks lined the streets, jostling each other to get a better view of the black who was rapidly becoming one of the most talked about men in the world.

The laborers, wearing their Sunday jackets over large white pantaloons, and their women, fresh and lovely in long thin cotton dresses and bright-checked bandannas, looked with wonder at their black brothers—at Toussaint's elite bodyguard in their scarlet cloaks and silver helmets, at the cavalry seated erect on their well-trained horses and at the proud military demeanor of the infantry. The soldiers of the infantry stood so straight and held their heads so high that, despite their rags, it was difficult to believe they had once been slaves, cowed by an overseer's whip. At Toussaint on his white stallion, with whites bowing and scraping all around him, the laborers stared and stared.

The procession stopped in the center of town, and Toussaint dismounted. White girls with baskets rushed forward and showered him with flowers and garlands. A beautiful Creole lady placed a laurel wreath on his head and kissed Toussaint on the cheek. The amused black leader returned the kiss.

Several white planters approached carrying a baldachin, a canopy made of rich silk. Toussaint's eyes narrowed as he recognized two planters who had been his persistent enemies. But now they were bowing and scraping like the rest of the whites. They tried to raise the baldachin over the black leader, but Toussaint, irritated at their hypocrisy, stepped aside and snapped, "Only God should walk under a baldachin with incense wafting toward Him."

The planters, taken aback by his refusal, explained that this was the way the city traditionally received governors. But Toussaint would have none of it, and on foot and uncovered by the canopy he accompanied the procession to the mayor's palace.

That night Port-au-Prince was filled with the sounds of celebrating. In the palace, Toussaint and his officers attended a sumptuous banquet followed by a ball. The lovely Creole ladies competed openly for the attentions of Toussaint, and he treated them all with a respectful courtliness.

The following day a religious service was given in Toussaint's honor. The black leader, wearing a more elaborate uniform than was his custom, was an impressive sight. The cuffs and collar of his light-blue coat were trimmed with gold and crimson, and on his shoulders were gold-braided epaulettes. Under his coat he wore a white silk blouse, frilled at the neck. A wide, tricolor sash encircled his waist, and a sword hung from his side. His three-plumed hat was adorned with the red cockade of the French Republic.

In the church, Toussaint sat in a place of honor on a thronelike chair. After the service and hymns the white mayor of Port-au-Prince mounted the pulpit and delivered a long eulogy honoring the black general.

Toussaint then mounted the pulpit, thanked the mayor and everyone for their kindness and proceeded to rebuke all the whites of Port-au-Prince for surrendering so willingly to the British.

"Your countryside is so uncultivated and bare it filled me with dismay on my journey here. One look at it should convince any reasonable man that you made a foolish mistake in joining the British. You had expected to gain much profit from such a move. Instead, you only lost!"

Taking hold of the pulpit, Toussaint leaned forward, visibly angry. "Will you property owners *never* learn that free men who are rewarded for their labor will produce far more than a shackled slave?"

Then he relaxed somewhat, and his voice softened. "But the age of fanaticism is past. Let us now work together to restore agriculture for the prosperity of Haiti and the well-being of all citizens."

When Toussaint finished his work in Port-au-Prince, he

returned to his headquarters in the North. The British still occupied Jérémie in the South and Môle St.-Nicholas in the North. Toussaint wanted to take these last two outposts without bloodshed. He began making diplomatic maneuvers to convince General Maitland to negotiate. At the same time, other parties were pressuring Maitland *not* to negotiate.

Events in Haiti had shaken the entire West Indies. The governor of Jamaica, a British colony in the Caribbean, was especially alarmed. Jamaica had about one quarter of a million slaves, and was only about 130 miles west of Haiti. If Toussaint got control of Haiti, he would surely try to free Jamaica's slaves. The governor begged Maitland to hold out, conjuring up terrible images of what could happen to British colonialism in the West Indies if he did not.

When Toussaint learned of the Jamaican governor's interference, he sent him an immediate warning. "May I remind you, my dear Governor, of the proximity of your colony to my beloved Haiti. A few thousand blacks could make the trip in canoes. Of course, I prefer *not* to intervene in the affairs of Jamaica. Perhaps, Governor, you will act in an equally wise manner."

The governor of Jamaica immediately communicated Toussaint's threat to Maitland. The British general now had to look at his position in a different light. The British owned a number of colonies in the West Indies. If Toussaint began stirring up slave revolts in these colonies, England might lose all its possessions in the Caribbean.

Maitland, prejudiced English gentleman that he was, still could not regard Toussaint as a brilliant general. But he had seen what his black army could do, and he had a healthy respect for that. He knew the British could no longer conquer the rest of Haiti. Was it worth risking the other colonies to hold onto a piece of Haiti? The answer was all too apparent.

Toussaint and Maitland met at the British headquarters

near Môle St.-Nicholas in August of 1798. As the black general entered the town surrounded by an imposing escort of white, black and mulatto officers, the guns of the British ships anchored in the bay boomed a salute. Maitland embraced Toussaint, and as trumpets blared, a thousand British soldiers marched in review before the black leader.

Toussaint and his officers were then escorted inside a huge tent, where a banquet table was set with an elaborately prepared lunch, costly wine and roses. Maitland drank to Toussaint's health and presented him with fabulous gifts in the name of King George III. Then he gave Toussaint his own gift, a beautifully wrought bronze cannon, saying, "I beg you to accept this modest gift as a token of my esteem and an expression of my gratitude for the humane treatment you gave British prisoners."

One of the greatest nations in the world was paying an elaborate tribute to the former slave. Such tributes are rarely without their purpose, and Toussaint waited patiently to see what Maitland was up to now.

After lunch the two generals retired to Maitland's tent to work out details of the British evacuation. When everything was settled, the British general leaned back and smiled at Toussaint. "Well, now I have a proposition to make you in the name of King George."

Toussaint waited, his mind racing over all the tricks Maitland might try.

"How would you like to see Haiti completely independent of France, ruled over by one man only." Maitland paused, smiled sweetly at Toussaint and added, "King Toussaint."

So that's your strategy, thought Toussaint. You couldn't win Haiti from France on the battlefield, so now you'll try to win her by trickery.

As Toussaint hesitated, Maitland hastened to assure him that he would receive full British protection. "I give you my word that a squadron of British ships will patrol Haiti day and night to protect you from French retaliation. All we ask in return is that you sign a treaty agreeing to trade exclusively with Great Britain."

Maitland's underestimation of him was so great, it almost made Toussaint smile. He knew royalist Britain would have no love for an independent black Haiti, even if it were a dictatorship. They would protect the colony only until the last Frenchmen had been ousted. Then they would walk grandly back in themselves. And that was exactly what the British planned.

Thanking Maitland for his offer, Toussaint said he had no interest in becoming king of Haiti. The trade agreement, however, was another matter. Toussaint desperately needed supplies, and France could not send them. Without guns, ammunition and heavy artillery he could not protect Haiti against future invasions from colonial powers—perhaps even from France.

Toussaint was unhappy over the political trend in France. With each new victory in Europe, the Republic moved farther away from the spirit of the French Revolution. The tide of reaction was on the rise. Toussaint watched with alarm as the enemies of the blacks, the wealthy French planters and seaport merchants, won back the power they had lost in the French government.

The Directory, which had succeeded the National Convention as France's governing body, showed no inclination yet to restore slavery, but Toussaint knew the planters and merchants were pushing in that direction. He could foresee that one day France might abandon her hard-won ideals and restore slavery in Haiti. His people must be prepared for such a terrible possibility. They must have arms.

But Toussaint did not want to sign an exclusive treaty with Britain. The United States, recognizing Toussaint as the real power in Haiti, had approached him about a secret trade treaty. Since that country was much closer than England, it would be a better source of arms in an emergency. Both treaties would have to be secret, of course. Haiti was supposed to trade only with France, and Britain was still France's enemy. It was a dangerous step, but Toussaint agreed to a nonexclusive trade treaty with Britain.

Almost another year was to pass before Toussaint signed the treaty and the last British soldier was evacuated. But the long, ill-fated British expedition in Haiti had come to its inglorious end. It was one of the worst colonial disasters in the history of the British Empire. Five years of fighting had taken the lives of forty thousand British soldiers, left many thousands more unfit for active duty and cost the Empire a fortune.

The French Republic owed quite a debt to its former slave. General Laveaux commented to his government, "If the colors of France continue to wave over Haiti, it is due solely to a black who seemed to have received a mission from Heaven to cement the shattered fragments."

Toussaint had done more than keep the French flag flying over Haiti. He had so drained the British army that for five years it could not muster enough strength to block France's advances in Europe. While England funneled off men and money into Haiti, the French Republic ran rampant over the rest of Europe.

France was not grateful. When Toussaint first began winning victories against the British, the French government marveled over the military genius of the "incredible black." But as Toussaint's power in the colony grew, they became increasingly nervous.

The leading black of Haiti was now a major political figure in the Western Hemisphere and the most powerful man in Haiti. Colonial powers all over the world were shaken by the success of the former slave they called "that black scoundrel." Now the French government also joined the chorus, for at the same time he was fighting the British for the French, Toussaint was taking bold steps toward self-rule for his people.

CHAPTER 8

TOUSSAINT did not want to break with France. He felt a loyalty to the democratic republic which had freed the slaves. Furthermore, Haiti was too weak to stand alone. But his first loyalty was to his people, and he was fearful for their future. If the blacks' liberty was to be assured, they must not only be armed; they must learn how to rule themselves. Then, if France became the enemy and tried to restore slavery, the blacks would force the French out and administer the colony themselves.

Slowly but inexorably, at the same time he was fighting the British invaders, Toussaint began moving toward self-rule for Haiti. The first step he took was the most painful.

General Laveaux, commander-in-chief and governor of Haiti, loved Toussaint and the blacks, but his first duty was to France. Toussaint would miss his friend sorely, but the welfare of his people came ahead of his personal happiness—ahead of everything else he wanted or cared about. Laveaux must return to France.

The black leader could not bear to offend his friend. Laveaux was old and no longer well. Toussaint approached him, very gently, with the request that he return to France as a deputy of Haiti. "Troubled days lie ahead, and I foresee much unpleasantness in store for you in Haiti," Toussaint warned Laveaux.

Putting his hand on Laveaux's shoulder, Toussaint said

softly, "Wouldn't you like a rest from all the troubles brewing in this wretched land? In France you would be safe from harm. And if you agree to act as a deputy, my people will be represented by someone devoted to their cause."

Laveaux remained quiet. He was beginning to get the true drift of Toussaint's meaning.

"France has many excellent men," Toussaint continued. "But how many of them are true friends of the blacks? How many can be relied on to remain loyal to our cause? I know of only one. There is no equal to you. My greatest wish now is to see you elected a deputy to France."

Laveaux understood. He sympathized with Toussaint's desire to see Haiti ruled by blacks, and he saw the conflicts that lay ahead if he remained. Not wanting to stand in the way of Toussaint and the blacks, he accepted the offer to make a dignified exit.

A few days later the black general bid the French aristocrat good-bye. It was a sad moment for both, but especially for Toussaint. Never again was he to find a friend whom he trusted so completely.

The most important French official in the colony was now Sonthonax, the commissioner who had declared emancipation. Toussaint and Sonthonax were very different men. The red-haired commissioner was an angry, emotional man, full of resentment toward aristocrats. Unlike the black leader, who had greater cause to dislike the aristocratic whites, Sonthonax nursed his anger to such a peak it clouded his vision of what was best for the colony. Toussaint wanted to correct injustices in an orderly, bloodless fashion by forcing the perpetrators to mend their ways. Sonthonax wanted to destroy injustice by smashing the perpetrators to pieces.

While the black leader worked hard to create peace and unity in the colony, Sonthonax fanned the flames of racial hatred. If a black complained that a white was mistreating him, the fair-skinned commissioner would roar, "Murder him!" Sonthonax was a valuable man, but his primitive, anarchistic views were disturbing to Toussaint.

In August of 1797, shortly after Laveaux left for France, Toussaint scored an important victory over the British, and Sonthonax chose the occasion to appoint Toussaint commander-in-chief of Haiti's forces. To celebrate the appointment, Sonthonax invited the black leader to dine at his home in Le Cap.

"You are now the most influential man in Haiti," said Sonthonax over coffee. "Your word is law, and no white dares defy you. The time is ripe. You must declare independence from France now!"

Amazed at such a suggestion coming from the French commissioner himself, Toussaint remained silent. Perhaps it was a trap. Perhaps Sonthonax was trying to discover if Toussaint entertained such a notion.

The commissioner, assuming Toussaint was thinking over the proposition, added, "Of course, you'll need my help, but I will give it to you. Together we'll build the first independent black republic. Haiti will be a living monument to equality for the masses!"

Still puzzled and suspicious, Toussaint asked, "And what role will the whites have in this republic?"

"The whites must be exterminated!" shouted Sonthonax. "There can be no security for the blacks in this colony until every white is deported or destroyed."

Toussaint had met many violent and ruthless men in his day, but a cold, premeditated plan to exterminate one's own people—could the man be serious? As he replied, Toussaint wondered if he were addressing a madman. "And if the colony cannot be safe until every white is removed, what would the commissioner advise me to do with him?"

Sonthonax was stunned. How could Toussaint categorize him with the other whites? Toussaint, eager to end the painful conversation and take his leave, broke the uncomfortable silence. "Your plan is not only hideously cruel but shortsighted as well. You say, 'Declare independence now.' Can you tell me how my people, who have been so long enslaved, can start administering a colony overnight? If all the whites were exterminated tomorrow, what chaos would follow! No, Commissioner, I intend to go on protecting the whites of Haiti."

Sonthonax leaped to his feet. "But they'll take over! They'll restore slavery!"

Toussaint would never admit his own fears about the whites to someone as irrational as Sonthonax. Making light of the commissioner's last remark, he asked, "Take over whom? Thousands of armed blacks who have tasted freedom? I think not, Commissioner. The real menace to our freedom now is external. We must defend ourselves against England, and for that we need arms. The whites will help us restore agriculture and buy arms."

Rising from his chair to leave, Toussaint said, "I detest violence and talk of bloodshed. It doesn't matter whose blood, whether friend or foe, white or black. It's all the same. Please don't bring this subject up again."

"It's finished," replied Sonthonax wearily and with a touch of bitterness.

By the time Toussaint left, his mind was made up. Sonthonax would have to go. His twisted ideas could stir up much racial hostility and internal strife at a time when harmony and unity were essential to the colony's future.

After some thought, the black leader sat down and wrote the commissioner a letter. He praised him for all his good works, and then went on to express his concern over the reactionary trend in France.

"Our liberty is in danger. Old voices—voices we had hoped

were stilled forever—are heard crying out for the restoration of 'order' in Haiti. Your work here has been invaluable, and we will miss your guiding hand. But now we need good friends like you in Paris. I beg you to make all haste before it is too late."

When Sonthonax read the letter, he grasped its real meaning immediately, and flew into a rage. "How can you treat me this way?" he replied in an angry letter to Toussaint. "Have you forgotten that it was I who proclaimed freedom for all slaves?"

Three days went by, and Sonthonax was still in Le Cap. Toussaint's patience ran out. He had not wanted to use force. But the commissioner obviously would not leave on his own.

At four o'clock the next morning, while the city of Le Cap slept, General Moyse and a dozen armed blacks rode slowly through the dark, drowsy streets. At the commissioner's home they dismounted and ordered the guard to waken Sonthonax. When the sleepy commissioner appeared, Moyse said, "The frigate *L'Indien* is in the harbor. She sets sail for France at one o'clock. If you're not aboard by noon, you'll be forcibly deported."

The news had spread, and hundreds of blacks were on hand to bid Sonthonax good-bye. The commissioner was their friend, and they were shocked and grieved that he was leaving. But if Toussaint said he must go, of course he must.

Toussaint made certain the commissioner's departure was dignified. He himself was at the harbor to bid him good-bye, as soldiers lined the quay, raising their swords in salute to the departing commissioner. When the frigate pulled up anchor and moved slowly out of the harbor, the guns of Le Cap's fort boomed in a final farewell. Sonthonax was gone.

"First Laveaux, now Sonthonax," mumbled Moyse, who stood next to Toussaint, his eyes on the ship receding in the distance. "How will they like this in France?"

Toussaint turned slowly and fixed Moyse with a cold,

warning stare. He did not like other people putting his own fears into words.

There was good reason to be concerned over France's reaction to Toussaint's high-handed treatment of her representatives. When Sonthonax arrived in Paris, he lost no time maligning the man who had ousted him from Haiti. "Toussaint's whole political career has been one long revolt against France!" he warned the Directory.

The French government, hitherto very suspicious, was now convinced. Toussaint was plotting for independence. But what could they do? Toussaint was still fighting the British. If they moved against him, he might go over to the British, and Haiti would be permanently lost. Somehow they had to check his power without alienating him. When the war in Europe was over, France would be free to deal with "that black scoundrel."

Months later, shortly after the British had surrendered, three French warships sailed into the harbor of Le Cap. Aboard one of the ships was Count d'Hédouville, a special agent sent by the Directory, and his party of administrative and military "experts."

Hédouville bore a message for Toussaint from the French government, confirming Toussaint's appointment as commander-in-chief, expressing its willingness to accept the deportation of Sonthonax and assuring Toussaint he would be able to work well with Hédouville for the good of Haiti and the Republic. The real purpose of the message was to quiet any fears Toussaint might have about Hédouville's mission, for the special agent had been instructed to do everything possible to check Toussaint's power without arousing his suspicions.

Toussaint and France, now separated by a deep distrust, were both playing a deceitful game of political diplomacy. The French soon learned the black leader was more than their match at the game.

Special agent Hédouville had fought bravely for the Republic, and loudly proclaimed his aversion to royalty and aristocracy. But in his heart he harbored many prejudices. It secretly galled him to see a former slave in a position of power. Before leaving France he had conferred with everyone he knew who had met Toussaint. "What kind of man is he? What is the secret of his power and success?" he asked them.

A French general replied, "Toussaint's influence on the blacks is extraordinary. With him on your side you can do everything. Without him, you can do nothing."

A planter warned Hédouville, "Toussaint misses nothing. He has the uncanny ability of reading the secret thoughts of anyone with whom he is dealing—friend or foe."

And a former commissioner said, "His power is so enormous that were he not the most virtuous of men he could easily abuse it."

With such advice, Hédouville should have had few illusions about the difficult task ahead of him. His prejudices were such, however, that from the moment he arrived he assumed a superior attitude that led him from one mistake to another, until the skilled and gifted diplomat finally fell right into the artful trap Toussaint had set.

Toussaint had a pretty good idea why Hédouville had been sent. What he did not know was how the special agent planned to carry out his task. Pretending to be delighted with the message from the Directory, Toussaint sent Hédouville his personal greetings and ordered that he be welcomed with all respect. Once the special agent was settled in Le Cap, Toussaint went to talk with him.

As they awaited Toussaint's arrival, Hédouville's administrative and military experts lounged about the conference room of the government palace discussing the famous black leader. Arrogant young men fresh from victorious battles in Europe, they regarded the whole fuss about "an old darky" to be absurd. The fact that the "old darky" had just trounced the British was insignificant. He was black and an ex-slave.

When Toussaint arrived, Hédouville hastened to greet him like an old and trusted ally. The black leader accepted the flowery welcome with his typical reserve and glanced about, scrutinizing the men in the room. As the two men talked, Hédouville's staff and Toussaint's officers stood by, eyeing each other with hostility.

The special agent, always the diplomat, tried to thaw the atmosphere with flattery. "Well," he began, "our country owes you a very great debt indeed. People are comparing you with the greatest military geniuses of all time!"

Bowing his head in recognition of the compliment, Toussaint replied, "My abilities, such as they are, are based on my love for Haiti and my unswerving loyalty to France."

Toussaint then briefed Hédouville on the many difficulties plaguing the colony. When he finished, he leaned back and sighed wearily. "I am grateful that you are here, Citizen Agent, to relieve me of some of my burden. It has been a long, arduous journey, and I'm feeling rather weary."

The admiral of the warship that brought Hédouville heard Toussaint's remark. Stepping forward, he bowed to Toussaint and said, "How flattered I'd be if Toussaint Louverture allowed me the honor of bringing him back to France aboard my ship. In France you would be given a hero's reception and the long rest you have so well earned."

Amazed and angered by such crude and undisguised rudeness, Toussaint replied, "Sir, no ship is big enough to carry me away from Haiti. If you wait for Toussaint Louverture to go to France, you will wait until that sapling outside the window is big enough to make a ship and carry me."

Hédouville filled the tense silence that followed with some flowery nonsense, and the blacks took their leave. Toussaint's suspicions had been confirmed. Hédouville and his haughty staff spelled trouble.

As he rode off with his officers, Toussaint wondered how he should deal with this new problem. The special agent was too clever to challenge his power openly. That he would try to undermine it, Toussaint had no doubt. He decided to wait until Hédouville showed his hand.

He did not have to wait long. Hédouville was soon meddling in everything and objecting to all Toussaint's moves to improve agriculture and the economy. He even tried to convince the blacks that Toussaint was conniving with the British to restore slavery. The relationship between the two men deteriorated rapidly.

Toussaint was still conducting negotiations with the British, and the agent wavered between two fears. One minute he worried that the former slave was not clever enough to deal with the British. Perhaps Maitland would dupe Toussaint at Haiti's (and France's) expense! The next minute he worried that Toussaint might be too clever and dupe the French. Perhaps he'll sign a secret treaty with the British! The agent, disturbed by the first thought and outraged by the second, decided to intervene and sent his own agent to Maitland, offering his own peace terms.

When Toussaint learned of Hédouville's interference, he went to Le Cap and angrily confronted the agent. "If you think me incapable of dealing with the English, why don't you say so openly? But no, you ignore my position as commander-in-chief and send a junior officer to undermine my power in treating with the British. If you have no confidence in me, how can we work together for the good of the colony?"

Hédouville did not like being criticized by anyone. Being criticized by a former slave was especially galling to him. "Are you trying to tell me how to deal with the British?" he shouted at Toussaint, trembling with anger. "Maitland is a very clever man. He could have duped you!"

"When the French army in Haiti faced disaster at the hands of the British, you were content to let me deal with the enemy alone," Toussaint accused him. "Now that my army has defeated the British, suddenly I'm too inexperienced to deal with them?"

"May I remind you, General, that it is in my power to dismiss you!" Hédouville shouted.

Having bumbled from one diplomatic *faux pas* to another, Hédouville was now playing his last card. He was openly threatening Toussaint's power and authority. It was what the black leader had been waiting for. "I believe, Citizen Agent, that you want very much to do just that. To save you the embarrassment such an act would cause, I hereby submit my resignation."

Toussaint then strode out of the room, leaving the experienced diplomat speechless. He had never dreamed it would be so easy.

The black leader retired to his plantation at Ennery, where Suzanne and his family now lived. The agent, delighted with the unexpected turn of events, immediately sent a report to the Directory, adding, "Now we must find a way to reduce the power of the black army. As long as the army remains strong, I cannot formally accept Toussaint's resignation. His men would revolt."

The French government had a brilliant scheme to get rid of Toussaint and the black army. In its confidential reply to Hédouville, the Directory suggested, "Perhaps we can persuade Toussaint to broaden his search for military laurels."

Hédouville was delighted with the Directory's plan, and immediately set the wheels in motion.

Soon thereafter an important representative of the French

government called on Toussaint at Ennery. Over a simple lunch prepared by Suzanne, he described to the "retired" black leader the miserable conditions of slaves in the British colony of Jamaica and in the United States. "France is concerned that slavery still exists in the New World. The people are demanding that all slavery be abolished. No one is more suited to the task than you, General. I am authorized to offer you the aid of an entire French fleet if you and your army will liberate the slaves of Jamaica and the United States."

Toussaint had learned to enjoy intrigue, and excelled at the game. He remained quiet, pretending to be thinking about the offer, but he immediately recognized the proposal for what it was. He knew if he succeeded in such an endeavor, it meant more glory and more territory for France. If he failed and his army was defeated, the threat of black power in Haiti would be over. Whether he won or lost, by the time he returned to Haiti, the French would have an iron grip on the colony again. But he quickly saw how he could turn France's proposition to his own advantage.

"It is flattering, indeed, to know that such a great and powerful country as France would entrust me with such an enormous task," Toussaint finally replied. "Of course, there are many things to consider. May I have some time to think it over?"

"Of course, of course, General," replied the French representative, convinced he had succeeded.

Toussaint lost no time in leaking the word out to the proper channels. The trade treaties with England and the United States had not yet been drawn up. Many of the terms were still to be worked out. A little scare could certainly work to his advantage when the final terms were agreed upon.

Word of France's scheme reached American and British

representatives in Haiti. At one time such a rumor would have struck government officials as highly amusing, but Toussaint and his army were no longer a laughing matter. If Toussaint did attack, the quarter of a million slaves in Jamaica would probably rise up and join him, as would the thousands of slaves on plantations in southern United States.

As Toussaint anticipated, the British and American representatives, alarmed by the rumor, made strong appeals to him to reject the proposal. In June of 1799 the black leader put his signature on a secret tripartite treaty with Great Britain and the United States. The treaty, granting the two countries equal trade privileges with the colony, was a very favorable one for Haiti. In return, Toussaint promised no expeditions would be sent out against either country or any of their possessions. The United States and Jamaica breathed easier.

Both England and the United States now treated Haiti as an independent nation, rather than a French colony, and Toussaint, rather than France's special agent, as Haiti's ruler.

Such treaties could not be kept secret for long, and when Hédouville learned about them, he nearly wept with frustration. "His signature is not legal!" he shouted to his staff. But he knew this was not true, for he had not yet formally accepted Toussaint's resignation.

France's scheme to get rid of Toussaint and the black army by trickery had failed. Hédouville decided to take his chances and simply order the army to disband. He moved fast, but the first step he took was a mistake. He tried to disband the regiment commanded by General Moyse. Hédouville had so little real contact with the blacks he did not know Moyse was the most popular man in the army.

When a detachment of French soldiers arrived at the fort

and demanded that the blacks lay down their arms, Moyse, a courageous, stubborn man who distrusted most whites, refused the order. An argument broke out, and the French soldiers opened fire. Several blacks were killed and the regiment scattered. Moyse, seriously wounded, barely escaped alive.

When news reached Le Cap, the blacks rose up in fury, and France's special agent found himself face to face with the threat of civil war. Toussaint had retired only because he knew that Hédouville, if left to his own devices, would make a mess of things. Now that the agent had fallen into his trap, the black leader did not hesitate.

"March on Le Cap and seize the fort!" Toussaint ordered Dessalines.

Then he instructed his soldiers to ride through the countryside, calling up the black laborers. From plantation to plantation, his men galloped, spreading the alarm, "Hédouville is disbanding the army! He wants to restore slavery! On to Le Cap!"

Tens of thousands of laborers dropped their work and, armed with spades, pitchforks and pickaxes, marched on the city. "Down with Hédouville!" they shouted as they marched through the streets.

Dessalines stormed Le Cap's fort, garrisoned by French militia, and began firing the cannon to instill fear in the hearts of Hédouville and his staff. He succeeded. The agent, his staff and all his supporters fled to safety aboard a French warship. While Hédouville and his arrogant young "experts" cowered below deck, the "old darky" who had been the butt of their jokes rode through the streets of Le Cap amid cheering throngs. The presence of Toussaint always meant one thing—the restoration of peace and order.

The black leader sent a message to the agent inviting him to return and promising no harm would come to him. But

Hédouville had seen the scope of Toussaint's power, and home and France seemed very appealing. The ship pulled up anchor and sailed away, leaving behind a triumphant Toussaint, his power now unfettered by scheming Frenchmen.

The next day Toussaint addressed the citizens of Le Cap in the public square.

"Agent Hédouville thought he could destroy the brave General Moyse and the Fifth Regiment. Did he not realize that behind them stood thousands of blacks who would avenge their deaths? Agent Hédouville tried to convince you that I am the enemy of liberty, that I sold out to the British. Who do you think values liberty more—Toussaint Louverture, former slave, or Count d'Hédouville, former Marquis and Chevalier of the Order of St. Louis?"

"Toussaint Louverture! Toussaint Louverture!" the people shouted.

"Before he left," Toussaint continued, "Hédouville said he would return at the head of an army and take Haiti. I don't want to fight France. I have fought too hard to preserve the colony for her. But if she attacks me, I will defend myself. Remember, there is only one Toussaint, and that is a name to make people tremble!"

Hédouville had worked hard to sow the seeds of dissent and undermine Toussaint's power. But the blacks had not been the main target of his poisonous propaganda, for the agent had quickly discovered the colony's most potentially explosive problem—the uneasy alliance between the mulattoes and the blacks.

Having found this weak spot in Toussaint's hold on the colony, Hédouville did all he could to divide the two races further. The poison he left behind continued to work for him. Even before Hédouville touched French shore, his evil conniving was to catapult Haiti into its most bloody war.

CHAPTER 9

AS long as the blacks and mulattoes were at each other's throats, the colony could never be strong. No one was more acutely aware of this than Toussaint, who devoted much energy to reducing the bitterness between the two races. Despite their differences, he and the mulatto leader Rigaud had managed to work well together . . . until Hédouville came along.

Hédouville had quickly discerned that the mulattoes resented the blacks and that Rigaud was jealous of Toussaint's power and prestige. The agent's task had been to check Toussaint's power without turning him against France. What better way to achieve this than to use the mulattoes? If he played his hand properly, Rigaud and his people would do the dirty work for him.

Little that went on in Haiti escaped Toussaint. He knew that Hédouville had been wooing Rigaud, but he believed that the mulatto leader, despite his faults, was at least clever. He would surely see Hédouville was merely trying to use him.

Hédouville's first act after boarding the warship had been to write a letter to Rigaud.

"General Toussaint Louverture has sold himself to the British and Americans. He has violated the most solemn agreements with France. Because of his ambition and perfidy, I am obliged to leave the colony. I hereby relieve you, General Rigaud, of any obligation to recognize Toussaint Louverture as your commander-in-chief, and instruct you to assume command."

The vain and power-hungry Rigaud was delighted with the letter, but he did not make it public. The memory of his last bid for power was still fresh. This time he would move more cautiously. He began by writing a letter to the black leader expressing his disapproval of Hédouville's ouster from the colony.

"You have struck a cruel blow against those of us whom the Revolution has helped to live again. Many fools have been saying we want independence. Now all France will believe it!"

After reading the mulatto's letter, Toussaint handed it to Moyse, commenting sadly, "It appears the agent succeeded. I did not think Rigaud would be so foolish."

Moyse read the letter, and slammed his fist on the table, shouting, "You must arrest him immediately!"

"No," replied Toussaint. "I need Rigaud. He is violent and excitable but he wages war courageously. If I arrest Rigaud, the mulattoes will only find another leader—perhaps a better leader. Rigaud at least is obvious. He gives free rein to his horse when he gallops, and shows his arm when he strikes. He is less dangerous than one who strikes but is never seen."

But Rigaud was stirring up considerable trouble, turning more and more mulattoes against the black leader. Toussaint had to do something. Once again he tried to resolve his difficulties with the mulattoes in a reasonable, peaceable way. He called a conference of all the black and mulatto leaders in Haiti.

His efforts at conciliation failed. While the conference was in progress, a riot broke out in a small town in the South, Rigaud's territory. Thirty blacks were arrested by the mulatto authorities and imprisoned in a windowless shed. The next day, when the jailor opened the door, he found thirty dead bodies. The building had been recently whitewashed, and the poisonous chemicals and lack of air choked the men to death.

An aide brought the news to Toussaint while he was sitting at the conference table. Furious, he turned on Rigaud. "Always the blacks! It is always the blacks who pay the penalty of these disorders. And always the disorders are deliberately provoked!"

Rigaud rose from his seat, his face contorted with rage.

"It is *you*," he said, pointing his finger at Toussaint, "not I who have betrayed the blacks. It is *you* who made a secret treaty with the royalist enemy of the Republic!"

"The treaty with England was in the interest of the colony," replied Toussaint coldly. "We need arms. As to France, I have made no breach with the Republic. In fact I have requested the French Commissioner Roume to leave his post in Santo Domingo and come to Haiti to replace Hédouville."

This was news to Rigaud and not good news. Unlike Hédouville, Roume was a great admirer of Toussaint's. He considered Toussaint the mainstay of French authority in Haiti and the most important peace-keeping factor in the colony. He felt the best way to keep the black leader loyal to France and prevent him from proclaiming independence was to cooperate with him fully. He was very critical of Hédouville's methods and sympathized with Toussaint for getting rid of him.

The sensible, mild-mannered Roume would never support Rigaud's bid for power. The mulatto leader had to act quickly. Leaning over the table toward Toussaint, he shouted, "You've gone too far! First Laveaux, then Sonthonax and now Hédouville. And having got rid of all them, *you* decide who's to be the next commissioner. Well, I don't like it and I don't accept it!"

Rigaud then stormed out of the room, followed by the other mulatto leaders. The next day he published Hédouville's letter relieving him of his obedience to Toussaint. Proclaiming his loyalty to the Republic, he denounced the black leader as a traitor and a "three-faced monster, betraying one by one Spain, England and France."

The mulattoes, already resentful of Toussaint's power, were only too eager to believe Rigaud and obey Hédouville, the true representative of France, by overthrowing Toussaint.

Toussaint of Haiti

They responded in mass to Rigaud's call to rally against the black leader.

Commissioner Roume had accepted Toussaint's invitation to replace Hédouville. In July of 1799, he declared Rigaud a rebel and an outlaw, and appealed to all colonists to stand by the black leader.

Toussaint feared no words could ward off the terrible menace of civil war now stalking the land. He foresaw better than anyone the horrors it would bring—black against mulatto, brother against brother, all the people who should be enjoying peace and freedom now that the British were gone, pitted against each other in a wasteful, useless war.

Despite the warnings and pleas of his advisers, Toussaint mounted his horse and headed south to Port-au-Prince, which had a large mulatto population.

When Toussaint came galloping into the city with his bodyguards, the mulattoes of Port-au-Prince were amazed but curious. From his horse Toussaint announced he would address the people in the church. The church filled quickly, and the black leader, standing on the pulpit, addressed the mulattoes:

"Mulattoes, from the beginning of the slave rebellion you have been betraying the blacks, your brothers. What do you want? As everybody knows, you want to rule Haiti! You want to eliminate the whites and enslave the blacks. Think carefully before you take such a step. Rigaud, the rebel and traitor, is lost! The hosts of liberty will crush him!"

The church was very quiet. Leaning forward, Toussaint said in a voice soft but menacing, "Mulattoes, I can see to the very bottom of your souls. You mean to revolt. But remember, when I leave here, my eye and arm will remain—my eye to watch you and my arm to reach out for you!"

But Toussaint's last, desperate attempt to put fear into the mulattoes failed. With four thousand men Rigaud attacked

Petit-Gôave, a coastal town in the South garrisoned by seven hundred black soldiers. The blacks were forced to retreat and narrowly escaped capture.

The "War of the Knives" had begun. It was to be the bloodiest and most tragic war the colony had yet seen.

Rigaud gained ground swiftly. Despite his accusations against Toussaint, he himself had been trading with the British and Americans, and his army had plenty of ammunition and supplies. The mulatto people, proud, courageous and determined, fought brilliantly, as though possessed.

The mulatto leader did not hesitate to use Toussaint's enemies, even those who were black. With lavish offers of promotions and wealth, he won over several of Toussaint's officers and a number of his soldiers. The Maroons, still suspicious of the black leader for supporting the hated French, fought with the mulattoes. But most blacks remained faithful to Toussaint, and the whites, because they knew him to be humane and just, sided with him almost to a man.

Toussaint did not anger easily. Once aroused, however, his fury was formidable. From the whites he expected trouble. But from his own people and the mulattoes, all his brothers, it was intolerable.

With typical speed, Toussaint dispatched his loyal officers and their armies to the various trouble spots of the colony. Dessalines marched to the West to take Port-au-Prince. Moyse went north to recapture Môle St.-Nicholas, which had rebelled and sided with Rigaud. Christope moved into Le Cap. Charles Belair, another of Toussaint's nephews and now one of his most trusted officers, was ordered to keep Rigaud busy. Toussaint himself swept through the North crushing revolts with such swiftness the rebels were thrown into a panic. In an amazingly short time, the uprising in the North was under control.

The black leader now headed to the South to take care of

Rigaud. To get there, he had to cross mountains invested with Maroons. Toussaint's soldiers kept a careful eye out for snipers as the army, strung out in a long line, made its way across the mountains, cavalry first and infantry last. As they moved slowly through a narrow pass with Toussaint at their head, several shots rang out. Toussaint's white physician, who rode by his side, fell dead from his horse.

A few hours later, as they came around a bend in the mountain trail, more shots rang out and a bullet took the plume off Toussaint's helmet. His escape from both these ambushes unscathed further convinced the people that he was "beloved of the African gods."

Before he could enter the South and attack Rigaud, Toussaint had to take Jacmel, the mulatto stronghold near the border between the Southern and Western provinces. This was a task to challenge the greatest of military geniuses. Located on the Caribbean coast, Jacmel was a natural fortress, with the sea on one side and a half circle of mountains on the land side. The fort was garrisoned by over four thousand mulattoes. Hidden batteries, blockhouses and other defenses made an assault by land impossible. Only an attack by sea could succeed. But Toussaint had no fleet. The other alternative was to cut off the mulattoes' supplies and starve them out.

Toussaint appealed to the British and Americans to stop delivering supplies to Rigaud, and both agreed. Then he settled down to wait. Somehow he managed to have siege guns transported from the West across the mountains, and day after day the big guns bombarded Jacmel. The black leader knew there were women and children in town. He sent a message pleading with them to leave and promising safe passage. No one left.

As the weeks went by and their food ran out, the mulattoes began eating their horses. When their horses had all been eaten, they ate their dogs and cats. Then they were reduced to rats, lizards, grass, leaves and anything their stomachs would tolerate. The soldiers still had gunpowder, but no more cannonballs. Loading their cannons with rocks and pebbles, they continued to fight. They were weak and starving, but they held on valiantly. They were confident Rigaud would soon appear with reinforcements.

Rigaud did not appear, and finally General Pétion, the mulatto commander, decided all civilians must leave. Toussaint had promised them safe passage, and the black leader had a reputation for keeping his word. Starving women, children and old men filed out of town unharmed. The black leader ordered them to be fed and sent without harm into the interior.

At last the mulattoes' gunpowder ran out. With it went all hope of defending the town. Too proud to surrender, General Pétion issued a last, desperate order to the remnants of his starving men. On the first moonless night they crept quietly out of the fort and tried to cut their way through Dessalines' line. But the all-knowing Toussaint learned of the maneuver, and Dessalines was ready. Only a few of the mulattoes escaped death or capture.

The siege was over. It had lasted five months, and was one of the most dramatic and heroic defenses in history. And where was Rigaud while his people hung on so courageously, waiting for him to appear?

During the siege of Jacmel, Rigaud was engrossed in matters of love—honeymooning with his new wife. He knew Jacmel was under siege, but he regarded Jacmel as impregnable. All his people had to do was hold out until Hédouville sent assistance, which Rigaud expected any day. Meanwhile, they didn't really need him, and his new wife was so charming . . .

As the mulattoes defended their town with an almost fanatical tenacity, Rigaud and his wife danced through the night, attending one ball after another in Les Cayes, a coastal town in the South where Rigaud had his headquarters. Not until he heard that Jacmel had fallen did the mulatto leader wake up. "That monster thirsting for human blood! That executor of Jacmel!" he shouted of Toussaint.

Rigaud immediately issued a proclamation to his people:

"If Toussaint Louverture is mad enough to invade the South, I swear to you, fellow citizens, that he and his army will find themselves dead and buried before they have advanced two miles. Even the trees in the South will raise up their roots against him!"

In contrast to Rigaud's angry proclamation, Toussaint issued a calm, soothing invitation to all mulattoes:

"Citizens! Toussaint Louverture is merciful and humane. He stretches forth fatherly arms toward you and bears you no grudge. Even if Rigaud himself, who is to blame for all this trouble, comes to me in good faith and admits his mistake, he will be received. But if Rigaud remains stubborn and does not take advantage of my offer, do not let it prevent you, fathers and mothers of families, from coming to me."

The black leader's proclamation impressed the mulatto people. Rigaud had let them down, and they were disillusioned with him. By contrast Toussaint seemed steadfast and trustworthy. He did not dance through the night while his people were dying. The mulatto people were tired of fighting. Toussaint offered them peace and forgiveness. They wanted to surrender.

Rigaud refused. Instead he ordered resistance unto death. Many of his soldiers deserted, but most remained loyal and obeyed. Soldiers on both sides fought savagely, gripped by the intense fury and hatred that marks civil wars, wars in which brother is pitted against brother. Overcome with rage, the mulattoes and blacks often dropped their muskets and fought with knives, giving the name "War of the Knives" to the conflict.

Rigaud's soldiers knew the mulatto population no longer

supported them. This made them so angry and resentful they began massacring the very people they had set out to defend. The grumbling against Rigaud and his soldiers grew louder.

Rigaud's situation grew increasingly hopeless, and he became depressed and demoralized. For days he would lose himself in apathy and self-pity, often drinking to excess. Then suddenly, seized with determination, he would launch an offensive that seemed to have no purpose other than costing lives.

Toussaint knew, even if Rigaud didn't, that the mulatto leader was beaten, and requested a French general to act as a peacemaker.

General Vincent and Toussaint were old friends. A man of character and principle, singularly free of all prejudice, the white general openly admired and respected the black leader, of whom he said, "Nobody can approach Toussaint without fear or leave him without emotion." Vincent often disagreed with the black leader and never hesitated to say so, but he defended him against his critics right to the end.

The French general agreed to try and persuade Rigaud to surrender, and he journeyed south to meet Rigaud at Les Cayes. The war-weary mulattoes of the town welcomed the representative of France, but Rigaud's soldiers eyed him with suspicion and hostility.

General Vincent and his aides, surrounded by mulatto soldiers, were escorted to the conference room of Rigaud's headquarters and left there alone to wait for the mulatto leader. In a few minutes the door flew open, and Rigaud, wild-eyed and like a man distracted, stood in the doorway. He wore a green uniform, with a sword at his side and pistols in his belt. Gripped tightly in his hand was the handle of a dagger, the blade hidden under his sleeve.

As the French general and his aides reached for their weapons, Rigaud strode toward Vincent, shouting in a high, shrill voice. "How can you cheat me like this? Toussaint is the traitor to France, not me. Why do you side with him, that slave to the royalists, that ungrateful wretch?"

Vincent returned his sword to its sheath, and spoke to Rigaud very softly. "I side with no man, only with France. It is my duty to see that an honorable peace is brought about for the good of all, not just one man or one race."

As he listened, Rigaud chewed on his handkerchief and looked nervously about the room, like a trapped animal. "I won't surrender!" he interrupted Vincent. "I'll kill myself before I give in to that traitor!"

Turning his back on Vincent, Rigaud stalked out of the room, and the mulatto soldiers informed the French general the conference was over.

When Vincent returned with the news, Toussaint was saddened and disappointed. Regretfully, he ordered Dessalines to march on Les Cayes.

Learning Dessalines was coming, Rigaud ordered his soldiers to smear all the houses in the town with tar so that the touch of a torch would send all of Les Cayes up in flames. Then, rushing to the arsenal, he ordered the officer in charge to blow it up.

But the mulattoes of the town did not want their homes burned down and the arsenal blown up. Faced with mass resistance from his own people, Rigaud was forced to accept the hopelessness of his situation. He refused, however, to surrender to Toussaint.

On a sultry day in August of 1800, Rigaud set sail for France.

As the defeated Rigaud sailed away from Haiti, a victorious Toussaint entered Les Cayes. Now, even Rigaud's most faithful supporters greeted the black leader with joy and relief.

Toussaint, as usual, promised "no reprisals." He declared

amnesty for all, and made a plea for peace and brotherhood between blacks and mulattoes. No property was to be confiscated, and no disciplinary action taken. All prisoners were released. Toussaint himself often appeared at camps and prisons, saying, "All is forgiven. You are free to return to your families. Be of good cheer."

One thing troubled Toussaint deeply. Hédouville had threatened to return at the head of an army. He had never come, and in waiting for him and counting on him, Rigaud had made a fatal error. But Toussaint knew that once the war in Europe ended, Hédouville might very well return as threatened.

The garrisons in the South were still manned by Rigaud's soldiers and officers. If Hédouville returned, these garrisons would welcome him with open arms. Toussaint decided these troops must be purged and untrustworthy officers removed from the ranks.

Toussaint had promised the mulattoes no reprisals, but the man who had always been true to his word failed to keep this promise. The step he now took was to become an indelible blemish on an otherwise exceptionally humane and distinguished career. Toussaint put Dessalines in charge of purging the mulatto troops.

Dessalines was a brilliant general. In battle he fought so fiercely and with such cunning and determination, the blacks called him "the Tiger." But he was also cruel and tyrannical and completely devoid of any moral values.

Toussaint knew Dessalines' character well. He should at least have commanded him to use moderation and then supervised his actions. Instead, Toussaint merely recommended moderation, and then turned his attention to other matters. His failure to foresee what would happen was one of the most tragic errors of his career.

Left to his own devices, Dessalines carried out what he

considered to be a proper purge. It would be better defined as a bloodbath. He and his soldiers massacred hundreds of prisoners, executed officers and put to death scores of prominent mulattoes throughout the South.

One day a number of mulatto officers were led into a field by Dessalines' soldiers and bayoneted to death. After the soldiers left, one badly wounded mulatto officer managed to crawl out of the field. Some blacks living in a cabin nearby found the mulatto and carried him home, where they nursed his wounds. Barely conscious, the officer told them of the massacre.

The next day the black woman who dressed the officer's wounds went to Toussaint's temporary headquarters. Throwing herself at his feet, she begged the black leader to forgive the mulatto.

"Forgive him?" Toussaint asked. "Who is he? What has he done?"

"I don't know," sobbed the woman, "but the soldiers tried to kill him. He'll die if you don't help him. The others are all dead in the field."

"What others? What field?" Toussaint asked, almost beside himself now.

The woman, realizing to her amazement that Toussaint knew nothing of the massacre, slowly recounted the officer's bloody tale. Stunned, Toussaint covered his face with his hands and wept. When he regained control of himself, he thanked the woman for coming. "My personal physician will accompany you home and tend to the wounded man."

As she left, the stricken Toussaint looked at his aides. Normally he would have criticized them sharply for not keeping him informed. But he was honest enough to know he could not blame them. He alone was responsible for putting Dessalines in charge of the purge. Shaking his head in bewilderment, he said, "I did not want this. I told Dessalines to prune the tree, not uproot it. Doesn't he realize such excesses will destroy liberty faster than all the treacherous plots of the enemy?"

Toussaint reprimanded Dessalines severely, and ordered all executions stopped at once. But the damage had been done. When he toured the South to see that his orders were carried out and the mulattoes well treated, Toussaint was met everywhere with coldness and distrust. His reputation as a humane conqueror who never broke his word—a reputation he had been justly proud of—had been soiled. The mulattoes would not easily forgive.

But the black leader had even worse troubles on his hands now than the resentment of the mulattoes. In France the Directory had been overthrown and a Consulate set up. Holding the title of First Consul of France was the military genius responsible for the upheaval, a brilliant power-hungry man with grandiose dreams of conquest and glory—Napoleon Bonaparte.

Napoleon was a cold and ruthless dictator. The French masses, who in their brief taste of power had demanded an end to oppression and tyranny, now huddled in silent fear, cowed by the fearsome Napoleon.

A man of many prejudices, well-known for his hatred of blacks, the First Consul was infuriated with Toussaint's rise to power. He was also enormously irritated by the black leader's worldwide prestige. Why, people were even calling Toussaint "the Bonaparte of the Antilles"—imagine comparing a black man and a former slave to him, the incomparable Napoleon!

The First Consul was still too busy with his European campaigns to deal with Haiti, but the little colony and Toussaint were first on his list of things to deal with once peace came.

Toussaint was not one to underestimate the enemy. He knew he had cause to be apprehensive.

CHAPTER 10

THE outcome of the "War of the Knives" disappointed Napoleon. He had hoped the blacks and mulattoes would destroy themselves. Then the whites would once again control Haiti.

When Rigaud arrived in France, he expected to be warmly welcomed and comforted. Instead he found himself face to face with an icy First Consul. Napoleon listened patiently to Rigaud's long tale of woe, and then said, "General, I can find only one fault with you—you have lost."

Shortly after becoming First Consul, Napoleon had called together the planters, seaport merchants and other rich bourgeois who supported him. "What is the most prosperous way to run the colonies?" he asked them.

"Slavery is the only profitable way to run the colonies," replied the men, whose only goals were order and profit.

"Then by all means we must restore slavery," said Napoleon.

But Napoleon had to move slowly. His own power was not yet great enough simply to invade the French colonies even if he could spare the troops to do it, which he could not. In the case of Haiti he had to be especially cautious. Toussaint's power, which France had failed to check, could not be ignored. The First Consul decided that for the time being he would play along with "the black scoundrel."

When Toussaint's agents in France warned him that the former slaveowners were pressing Napoleon to restore slavery, he sat down and penned an eloquent warning to the new First Consul:

"I am fully aware of what is being plotted in France. The

enemies of our liberty are quietly preparing a storm. Do not think that we who have known the blessing of liberty will stand by calmly while it is snatched away. You may find the blacks buried under the rubble of a country destroyed in the fight for liberty, but never again will you find them in chains."

Napoleon sent a representative to Haiti to placate the black leader. The representative read a proclamation signed by Napoleon guaranteeing the liberty and equality of the blacks and then informed Toussaint that the First Consul wanted Haiti's flag to be inscribed with a motto crediting the blacks' liberty to France.

"It is not to France that the blacks owe their freedom, but to their own valor!" responded Toussaint angrily. "We want no gratuitous concessions of liberty. We want recognition of the principle that no man—whether he be brown, black or white —can be the property of any other man. I refuse to put that inscription on the flag!"

Toussaint was not placated by Napoleon's representative. The black leader felt that the need to unify and strengthen Haiti was even more urgent now. With that aim in mind, he turned his eyes east, to the colony of Santo Domingo.

Since the Spanish colony had been ceded to France, the Republic had completely neglected it. Five years later the colony was still garrisoned by Spaniards, and slavery continued to be practiced there. Toussaint wanted to free those slaves. He also wanted to remove the threat posed by Haiti's entire eastern border being exposed. If a French invasion did come, troops could land in Santo Domingo and attack Haiti from all along her border with the Spanish colony.

The black leader decided to annex Santo Domingo. That would put the entire island under his control and make conquest by the French far more difficult. Having made this decision, he went to see Commissioner Roume.

Toussaint of Haiti

"The Spaniards are kidnapping blacks from Haiti and selling them as slaves to other colonies," Toussaint advised Roume. "We must put an end to this outrageous practice. I want you to issue a decree authorizing me to occupy Santo Domingo."

What Toussaint said about kidnapping blacks was true, but he was using it mainly as a pretext and Roume realized this. The commissioner, once such an enthusiastic supporter of Toussaint, had for some time now suspected the black leader was not the loyal, devoted servant of France he made himself out to be. Now he wanted to control Santo Domingo! It must be true, thought Roume. Toussaint wants independence!

More horrified by his own thoughts than Toussaint's words, Roume burst out, "I will not issue such a decree! I'll be cut into pieces before authorizing such a move!"

The black leader had not expected Roume to be happy about his request, but he was unprepared for such an outburst from the mild-mannered commissioner.

"If you don't sign such a decree, I shall enter Spanish territory with fire and sword," warned Toussaint.

"No!" roared Roume, storming out of the room.

Toussaint then called on General Moyse. "Roume refuses to authorize the decree. Perhaps if the people make their voices heard, he will change his mind. I'm leaving Le Cap tomorrow to attend to some business in Gonaïves. While I'm gone, will you see to it that the people are informed of the situation?"

Moyse understood Toussaint's meaning well. Soon from one end of the North to the other, angry voices were demanding, "Put a stop to the slave traffic!"

Toussaint's power was now so great he could unleash popular uprisings at will. When Roume still refused to sign, thousands of laborers left their plantations and marched toward Le Cap.

109

The citizens of the city urged Roume to meet the marchers outside the city and try to reason with them. Roume agreed, and soon the commissioner was face to face with thousands of angry laborers demanding the annexation of Santo Domingo. They were obviously in no mood to be reasoned with, but Roume, despite his mildness, was a man of conviction and not easily intimidated.

"I will not sign!" he shouted to the crowd. "If I have to choose between being sacrificed and authorizing this new war, I choose sacrifice."

An angry marcher broke from the crowd and rushed toward Roume with his sword drawn.

"Go ahead and strike!" Roume cried. "Strike hard! France will avenge me!"

But Toussaint had issued strict orders that Roume must not be touched, and the marcher was merely bluffing. Instead of striking Roume, he ordered his arrest. The commissioner and his aides were locked up in an empty chicken coop, and the laborers settled down to wait.

Toussaint remained in Gonaïves for several days, feigning ignorance of this terrible insult to the representative of France. Then he rushed to the scene, "scolded" the crowd and freed Roume.

"I was just informed of this dreadful indignity to your person," said Toussaint, who could be a brilliant actor when he wanted to be. "I rushed here immediately, but I'm too late. The crowd is already out of control. It will be impossible now to stop them from marching on Le Cap!"

Weary and somewhat ill from his stay in the chicken coop, the discouraged Roume finally admitted defeat. "All right, I'll sign," he agreed.

Toussaint handed the commissioner a pen and then rode away, in his pocket a decree signed by the representative of France authorizing him to annex Santo Domingo.

Hoping, as always, to avoid violence, Toussaint sent General Agé, his white chief of staff, to confer with Don Joachim García, who was still governor of Santo Domingo. But Roume's messenger got to Don García first, and before Agé arrived the governor had learned of Toussaint's plan and been advised by Roume to resist.

The governor was beside himself. "What! Santo Domingo occupied by a black army! The ancient city of Columbus ruled by a former slave? Never! Never!"

When Agé arrived in Santo Domingo's capital city (also named Santo Domingo), he found an angry and aroused populace. Mobs shouting insults surrounded him, and just as stones began flying, Don García arrived. Agé was whisked into the governor's carriage and escorted at top speed to the border.

It did not require any guessing on Toussaint's part to figure out who was responsible for Agé's reception. Roume openly expressed his satisfaction with events and publicly revoked the decree, citing Spanish resistance as his reason.

Before sunrise the next morning, a coach and a company of dragoons pulled up in front of Roume's home. General Moyse dismounted, spoke to the guard and was admitted inside. Soon a sleepy-eyed Roume appeared, demanding an explanation.

"I have orders to escort you and your family to the Dupuy plantation at Dondon," said Moyse to the commissioner. "All the preparations have been made, and I'm sure you and your family will be very comfortable there."

Roume protested, threatened and then pleaded. Moyse was polite but firm. When the sun finally rose over Le Cap, a carriage surrounded by dragoons could be seen heading toward the city limits. Inside the carriage a sad Roume was reassuring his mulatto wife and frightened daughter that Toussaint would never permit any harm to come to them. And Toussaint never did. Roume and his family lived a peaceful if restricted life at

Dondon for many months before the black leader arranged for their return to France.

Napoleon was enraged but impotent. He had to swallow his fury and accept the return of yet another French representative. Nor could he prevent Toussaint from annexing Santo Domingo. But when the time came, he would make that "gilded African" pay for his insolence and insults to France.

After Roume's departure from Le Cap, Toussaint made one last effort to take the Spanish colony without bloodshed. He wrote to Don García that he was sending General Moyse to take over the government. "I hope his visit will not be marred as was General Agé's, and that you will receive him peaceably."

But Don García was a proud Spaniard. He was not about to let Toussaint's threats cow him into surrendering.

The blacks marched again. One Spanish town after another fell to Toussaint's swiftly moving army. One evening, as the sky was streaked with the blazing colors of a tropical sunset, the black general and his army found themselves overlooking the capitol of Santo Domingo. From the city below they could hear the sounds of revelry. The daughter of General Herrara, the commander-in-chief of the Spanish army, had just been married, and the entire city was celebrating.

Herrara himself and many of his officers, their eyes bright and faces flushed, were toasting each other at a grand ball when a young officer burst in shouting, "General Herrara! General Herrara!"

The musicians stopped playing, and the dancers all stopped and turned. General Herrara rose from his table. "What is the meaning of this commotion, Lieutenant?"

Striding quickly toward the general, the young officer saluted and stammered, "Sir, Toussaint Louverture is here! He is camped in the hills above the city!"

Herrara stared intently at the officer, unable for a moment

to accept such an outrage. The ballroom was hushed, the gay dancers silent as waxworks.

"Sound the tocsin, Lieutenant!" shouted Herrara, coming out of his trance of disbelief. "We'll teach that insolent black a lesson he won't soon forget!"

The alarm sounded, and the men of the city drained their glasses of wine and rum, and rushed out of the cafés, ballrooms and banquet halls to chastise those insolent blacks. Beautiful Spanish women in lace mantillas stood on their balconies and in doorways waving good-bye and weeping. As the men marched away, they joked among themselves about teaching the blacks their lesson quickly so they could return to their merrymaking. "Don't go away!" they shouted to the women.

The Spaniards did return quickly, but they taught no lessons that night. They merely showed how fast they could learn. After one encounter with Toussaint's soldiers, they fled back to the city, leaving a number of prisoners behind.

Toussaint entered Santo Domingo city at the head of fourteen thousand troops in January of 1801. The proud Spaniards, recognizing how useless resistance would be, received the troops sullenly, and not a shot was fired. The black leader was now master of the entire island of Hispaniola, an area equivalent in size to Ireland.

The imposing appearance of the black army and its dignified commander amazed the Spaniards. The ruler of Haiti and Santo Domingo was wearing his blue general's uniform with gold-embroidered cuffs and large gold epaulettes. Over his shoulders hung a flesh-colored cloak made of the finest cloth. His high leather boots were equipped with spurs, and on his hat was a tricolor cockade and a panache in the colors of the French Republic. His aides and officers, too, were elegantly attired.

A pale Don García and several Spanish officials received

Toussaint's party at the government house and handed over the keys of the city.

The next day Toussaint went to work. He addressed proclamations to the people of the colony promising amnesty and saw to it that his promise was carried out. He proclaimed all slaves in the colony free. Ships preparing to leave the port of Santo Domingo with blacks kidnapped from Haiti were stopped, their grateful human cargo unloaded.

To the newly freed slaves, the black leader issued this warning: "Liberty does not mean the right to live in idleness or to create disorder."

Toussaint remained for some time in Santo Domingo, injecting life into the lazy colony where an earlier observer had seen "too little industry and too many monks."

Toussaint started new schools, promoted new industries, laid plans for an extensive road-building campaign, cleared the coasts of pirates and opened the ports to commerce with England and the United States. He issued laws forcing the sluggish Spaniards to develop their land, and soon Santo Domingo was exporting coffee, cocoa, sugar, ginger, cotton, indigo and many other crops.

The sleepy colonists had never seen such energy and purpose. For the first time all the people, rather than just the privileged few, began to enjoy prosperity. Expecting to be purged and suppressed by the victorious blacks, they instead found themselves freer and happier than they had ever been.

When he finished his work in Santo Domingo, Toussaint left his brother Paul in charge of the colony and returned to Haiti. There, peace having been restored, he devoted all his energies to building the foundation of his dream—an independent Negro state, the first in the world governed by blacks.

Toussaint had already wrought almost miraculous changes in Haiti. In less than ten years he had brought the powerful British army to its knees, suppressed the mulatto uprising, stopped the French from interfering and united the entire island under his rule. It had taken military genius and rare diplomatic skill to accomplish this. But his most difficult tasks still lay ahead. Powerful forces, some of the most powerful in the world, were solidly blocking the pathway to his dream. First among them was the small man who was casting such a giant shadow across the whole continent of Europe—Napoleon Bonaparte.

In the year 1801 slavery was still practiced in many parts of the world, and viewed with tolerance or indifference in the rest. The United States, which had declared all men free and equal, had not lived up to her own motto. The Civil War was still about sixty years away, and another hundred years would find the blacks still struggling.

Whites everywhere clung stubbornly to the myth that blacks were inferior, unable to guide their own destinies. Such a world would scarcely welcome the emergence of a free and progressive black nation. Toussaint knew that even if Haiti won independence, it would have to stand alone in a hostile world eager to see it flounder.

For a black Haiti to survive and prosper in such an atmosphere, years of careful planning were needed. To declare independence before Haiti was ready would be disastrous. Toussaint knew his people had a long road to travel and many sacrifices to make before they could stand alone against France or any other powerful colonial country.

His dream would not be realized in a day, perhaps not even in his lifetime. He worried that if he died, there would be no one to carry out the monumental task he had begun. And the war in Europe could end very soon. There was no time to waste.

Like a man with only weeks to live, Toussaint threw all his energies into forging the nation of his dream—a progressive black state that would be a model of enlightenment and a challenge to white colonialists throughout the world.

CHAPTER 11

TEN years of war and rebellion had devastated the colony of Haiti. Only about ten thousand whites remained. The rest had fled or been killed. Many mulattoes had also been slain, but, as Toussaint said, it was the blacks who suffered most. Nearly one third of the half-million population, or almost 170,000 blacks, had perished.

Most of the plantations were still in ruins. Agriculture was in sad disarray, and the economy wobbly. Marauders roamed the countryside, preying on whites and blacks alike. Many blacks, sick of bloodshed, violence and the excesses of slavery, wanted nothing more than to be left alone, to exist only for themselves and their families. Toussaint had an almost impossible job ahead of him.

The most urgent problem was agriculture, upon which Haiti's economy rested. Toussaint continued to invite planters to return and run their plantations, but now he warned them, "If you do not return, your property will be confiscated."

All the planters who remained or returned were obliged to pay one fourth of their plantation's revenue to the laborers working in the fields and one fourth to the government. About two thirds of the planters either had died or refused to return. The government took over these plantations, putting a military officer in charge. The next problem was to get more laborers to cultivate the fields.

After Sonthonax abolished slavery, many of the blacks left the plantations and returned to their ancestral habits. They built small dwellings, used a minimum of clothing and cultivated little plots, raising only enough crops to survive. Weary from a lifetime of exhausting labor, few of them relished the prospect of hard work. Toussaint sympathized with them thoroughly. He dreaded the prospect of forcing them to return to the hated plantations. They would look on it as a partial return to slavery, and it would cost him much popularity. For a long time he had resisted such a step, experimenting with other systems. But these had all failed, and it was painfully clear that only the large plantations could raise enough crops for exports. To obtain revenue for military supplies, Haiti needed an abundance of export crops.

Regretfully, Toussaint issued a drastic decree forbidding the cultivation of small plots of land. The blacks who had left the plantations were forced to return to them as paid laborers.

Toussaint then instituted a form of military rule at all plantations. The laborers who already were working on plantations had tended to move from plantation to plantation, seeking better working conditions. Often, when they had saved enough money, they stopped working altogether until their money was gone. This disrupted progress on the plantations, and Toussaint issued a decree to prevent such practices.

His decrees were dictatorial, and Toussaint did not like them any more than his people did. But he knew all their liberties were worth nothing as long as the colony was weak. Freedom would be but a memory if Haiti could not defend itself. Forced labor was at least preferable to the restoration of slavery.

Toussaint was stern with his people, but he was equally hard on the plantation owners. When he heard the planters were trying to take advantage of his new decrees, he was infuriated, and immediately issued a harsh warning to them.

Since the laborers' pay was based on a percentage of their

plantation's revenue, the blacks now had an incentive to work. As a result of this and their improved living conditions, they were vastly more productive than they had been as slaves when they worked much longer hours. Their life was not idyllic, but it was a considerable improvement over slavery. And they could look forward to the future, when the colony would be back on its feet and life would be better.

Toussaint's strict measures regarding agriculture were met with grumbling on all sides. The planters ranted and raved because they could keep only one half of their plantation's revenue. Laborers complained they weren't free. Where was the liberty they had fought so hard for?

"Here is your liberty!" replied Toussaint, grabbing a musket and waving it at them.

The black leader was trying to convince them that to protect their liberty they had to have arms, and to buy arms they needed money—the money that came from exporting the crops they were cultivating. Not all the laborers were satisfied with Toussaint's answers, but none dared defy him. Nor did the planters, for if they disobeyed the decrees, their property was confiscated.

As a result of Toussaint's policies, Haiti was soon producing two thirds the amount of crops the colony had yielded in a good year before the slave rebellion. With the revival of agriculture, economic prosperity returned.

Toussaint reorganized Haiti's administration, simplified the old cumbersome tax system, did away with abuse and fraud and gave the *gourde*, Haiti's unit of money, a uniform value throughout the island. He created new courts based on French law, and for the first time the blacks received equal justice with the whites.

With the return of prosperity, Toussaint was able to build bridges, roads, hospitals and schools. In Le Cap he constructed many fine buildings and a huge monument to commemorate the abolition of slavery. The government palace was tastefully remodeled. The new and elegant Hôtel de la République, built by blacks and whites together, could hold its own with the finest hotels anywhere in the world.

Former slaves held high administrative posts, often with an experienced white as their adviser. Although Toussaint's army was primarily black, he had on his staff many white advisers. When word got out that Toussaint would appoint whites, he was overwhelmed with office-seekers. But important positions were given solely on the basis of merit, and those whites who tried to gain favor with Toussaint through flattery failed utterly.

As Haiti changed and progressed, the blacks began to take a pride in the colony, their work and themselves. Many black generals, officers, administrators and merchants became quite wealthy, and purchased mansions in town which they furnished luxuriously. Having spent much of their lives in rags, they now dressed with great care, and the black women proved themselves rivals to the most exotic mulatto beauty. Their homes were the scene of many sumptuous banquets and balls, and these were attended by whites and mulattoes as well as blacks.

Schools were established throughout Haiti, and poor blacks learned a trade and how to read and write, all at the government's expense. Toussaint, determined that his people would become as cultured and sophisticated as any French citizen, did everything he could to encourage learning and self-improvement.

The practice of Catholicism was encouraged, and soldiers and officers were required to attend services. Voodooism was outlawed, and anyone caught taking part in a ritual was beaten with a cane. But despite the drastic measures Toussaint took to eliminate it, voodooism did not die in Haiti.

Theaters were reopened, and former slaves who had never been near a stage in their life displayed impressive talent. Free from the deadening propaganda of white superiority, they began to find and express their true selves in art.

The blacks lived fully. They worked hard, married and bore children. The children went to schools where they learned to be proud to be black. Music, no longer so sad, was everywhere.

Toussaint himself hurried back and forth between various parts of Haiti and his plantation at Ennery. When he returned home, he would be greeted warmly by Suzanne, his stepmother and his youngest son, Saint-Jean. His older son and stepson had been sent to school in Paris, and Pierre Baptiste, his godfather, lived quietly in Le Cap, refusing any special honors or attentions.

Suzanne, unchanged by all the wealth, fame and power that had come to the slave she married, was as unaffected and good-natured as ever. Devoted to her family, she remained quietly in the background carrying out her domestic duties, and to Toussaint she was like a restful haven after the storm.

But even at home Toussaint did not rest. He always rose at dawn and began his day with morning prayers and then a bath, during which he read any correspondence his aide had placed on a table beside the tub. He ate simple food, preferring fruit, vegetables and maize cakes, and rarely drank wine.

After breakfast he would ride about the plantation, talking to his foremen, watching the laborers work and giving a steady stream of advice. It was his ambition to make his plantation a model for all the other plantations in Haiti to follow.

Then one day he would be gone, deliberately making his destination mysterious. Starting out in a carriage surrounded by guards, he would travel several miles, then stop the carriage,

Toussaint of Haiti

mount his horse and dash off in the opposite direction, followed by only a few bodyguards.

No one knew when and where he would turn up. As in battle he seemed to be everywhere at once, and generally where least expected. He kept the whole island on its toes.

Toussaint made numerous inspection tours to all parts of Haiti. On a typical tour he might stop at a fort, check its fortifications, review the troops, then rush off to a cotton plantation, ride through the fields, talk to the manager and then go on to the cane fields. Along the way he would examine the banana trees, look over some fields planted with spices and, spotting a grove of coffee trees, dismount, bite into a bean and estimate the crop's yield and quality. Passing a grove of guava trees, he would stop and sniff the air. The fragrant, perfume-like smell told him the yellow fruits were ready for picking.

Then on to a village, where he would inspect the schools, give out scholarship prizes, talk to officials, listen to the people's grievances, settle disputes and be off again, leaving behind a general calm. The people, hearing he was in town, would rush to greet him, the black women lifting up their children so they could see a great man of their own race.

During these rigorous trips, Toussaint often covered as many as 125 miles a day, changing horses frequently at the numerous thoroughbred stables he maintained throughout Haiti. When he returned, he was generally alone, for no aide could keep up with him.

Complete master of his body, Toussaint frequently slept only two hours a night and could go for two or three days with no sleep at all. When he was not in a town, he slept in the open field, fully dressed, with his sword at his side. Messengers arriving at all hours of the night were surprised to find the commander-in-chief fully alert and ready to receive them.

Sometimes he would go for days, eating and drinking nothing but a little fruit and water. Like any man in power, he had many enemies and had to take precautions against being poisoned. When he stayed in the villages, he would allow only certain elderly black women whom he trusted to cook for him.

Despite his strenuous schedule and the urgency he applied to all tasks, Toussaint never neglected the colony's touchy racial problem. He knew how difficult it was for the whites and mulattoes to be ruled by blacks, and he did all he could to ease their hurt pride. He knew too that Haiti could never achieve peace and prosperity as long as the three races remained hostile and separate, divided by the artificial boundaries of racism. His dream for Haiti did not exclude the white and mulatto minorities. The blacks would rule, but the whites and mulattoes must have equal rights. Haiti was to be a truly integrated society where different races would live side by side in mutual respect and harmony.

Toussaint's handling of the problem was so skillful and sensitive that soon whites, blacks and mulattoes were all mingling politically and socially. Under his administration racial barriers crumbled so fast that the French General Vincent exclaimed, "Races melt beneath his hand!" The black leader accomplished so much in such a short time he left the world gasping.

Toussaint also recognized the diplomatic importance of social receptions—or "circles," as they were called in Haiti—and the government palace at Le Cap was the scene of many such affairs.

Often, when a reception was over and the last guest gone, Toussaint would retire to his study and ring for his secretaries. The black leader's energy and capacity for work were so great he exhausted everyone—his aides, his agricultural inspectors, his engineers, his secretaries. To keep up with Toussaint as he worked through the night, five secretaries were needed. They took dictation from him and made final copies of his replies to correspondence. If a letter did not seem perfect to him, he would have it rewritten over and over until it contained the exact tone and meaning he desired. Despite this insistence on perfection, he managed to answer an average of two hundred letters a day. When the last letter was completed and his bleary-eyed secretaries had staggered off to bed, Toussaint would lie down himself, often for only two hours, before beginning another strenuous day.

One evening, after an informal circle, Toussaint invited some of his guests into his private study, something he did quite frequently. Among the guests were several distinguished whites, including Bernard Borgella, the mayor of Port-au-Prince, who was now also Toussaint's counselor. Toussaint and his guests relaxed in comfortable chairs and chatted about France, religion, agriculture, commerce and many other subjects. If any of the former slaves and slaveowners felt uneasy mingling socially, they did not show it.

When Toussaint decided it was time for the guests to leave, he rose from his chair. His guests rose also, and the black leader escorted them to the door. As he was bidding them good-night, Toussaint put his hand on Borgella's arm, "Would you mind remaining? I'd like to discuss something with you."

Unlike many of the whites, Borgella was not hypocritical in his attitude toward Toussaint. Although a wealthy planter himself, Borgella recognized that Toussaint was an extraordinary man, and he knew it was in the best interest of the entire colony to cooperate with the black leader. He was one of the few whites who remained loyal to Toussaint to the end.

When the two men returned to the study, Borgella noticed that Toussaint was unusually agitated. The black leader paced back and forth, his hands clasped behind his back. Finally, with a sigh, he dropped into a chair near Borgella and took a stone from his pocket. Collecting semiprecious stones was one of Toussaint's hobbies, and he often found it soothing just to hold a stone in his hand and contemplate its cool beauty.

Looking at the stone in his palm now, Toussaint said to Borgella, "I feel as if I have taken flight in the realm of eagles. I have to be careful. I must watch closely where I alight."

Clenching the stone tightly in his fist the black leader continued. "I must alight on rock! That rock will be a constitution, a constitution that will guarantee my people's liberty forever and my authority for as long as I live."

"A constitution?" Borgella gasped, picturing Napoleon's fury. "But, but France . . . Napoleon . . . Haiti is still a colonial possession!" he blurted out.

"Of course she is," Toussaint replied coolly. "I didn't say I want to declare independence. Haiti needs France. But Haiti also needs a constitution."

"What will France's role in Haiti's government be?" Borgella asked, fearing the answer.

"The French government will send commissioners to speak to me."

Borgella was now thoroughly confused, and his confusion was understandable, for Toussaint, in seeking self-rule for Haiti but dependence on France, was striving for a kind of political allegiance that did not exist then—an allegiance today known as dominion status. In anticipating such a status, Toussaint was far ahead of the other political leaders of his time. Self-rule and free trade for colonies were unheard of in those days. The world was not yet ready for Toussaint's progressive idea.

Poor Borgella was so perplexed he could only think to ask, "But you will submit the constitution for Napoleon's approval first?"

"It's no use," Toussaint said, knowing as well as Borgella that Napoleon would never approve it. "It is impossible for me to stop now. I feel as if some occult power which I cannot resist were forcing me on. I even have dreams of sailing to Africa with a thousand soldiers and putting an end to the entire slave trade! Just imagine—millions of blacks free at last!"

Borgella could not help but wonder what other plans Toussaint might have in mind that he *wasn't* confiding. If the black leader were to continue in the direction he was headed, an expedition to Africa was far from preposterous. Unknown to Borgella, Toussaint had already opened an account in an American bank. Such plans cost money.

Turning his thoughts back to the constitution, Borgella let out an audible sigh. He knew Toussaint too well to think he could change his mind. Although the black leader surrounded himself with advisers and listened carefully and thoughtfully to them, he always made up his own mind. And once it was made up, there were few men forceful enough to persuade him to change it.

Rising from his seat to indicate the interview was over, Toussaint asked, "Will you help me draw up a constitution for Haiti?"

"Yes, General," said Borgella, sighing again.

"And Father Molière will help us, too," said Toussaint, referring to a Catholic priest who was one of his closest advisers. "I'll contact him in the morning."

Before sunrise on July 7, 1801, the citizens of Le Cap were awakened by the tolling of bells and the roll of drums. The first constitution in Haiti's history was to be proclaimed at a public ceremony as soon as the sun rose.

By 5:00 A.M. the garrison of Le Cap stood at attention in the Place d'Armes, surrounded by a huge crowd of citizens waving French flags. The balconies of all the houses around the square were filled, and from each balcony a French flag waved gaily in the early morning breeze.

Toussaint, dressed in a simple blue and gold general's uniform, arrived at the head of a solemn procession composed of civil, military and church authorities. When the people saw the black leader, the entire square thundered with their cheers. The members of the procession seated themselves about the speaker's platform, which was decorated with flags and palm leaves. The bells and drums were quiet.

Borgella stepped up to the speaker's platform, read a formal announcement proclaiming the constitution and made a brief speech praising Toussaint and the historic occasion. Then he introduced the black leader, calling him "an extraordinary man who sprang like a phoenix from the ashes of revolution to devote his life to the defense of your country and your lives."

The cheering was so loud and prolonged when Toussaint rose that he could not begin speaking for several minutes. But the black leader did not look exhilarated or triumphant. The constitution was the boldest step he had yet taken toward self-rule for Haiti's blacks. Proclaiming it without Napoleon's approval was a very grave matter. In the midst of the gaiety the possible consequences of his deed weighed heavily on him.

When Toussaint addressed the people, he spoke simply. He explained what the constitution meant to each class of people, and reminded all citizens of their duty to protect the freedoms it guaranteed. He ended by reading the sections of the constitution that abolished slavery for all time and stated the right of all citizens, no matter what their color, to hold public office.

The black general was now the black consul. The former slave had truly reached the realm of eagles. But the summit is a lonely place to be—and it was especially lonely for a black man in the year 1801. Few were the men courageous enough to change places with the black who had just publicly defied France and the fearsome Napoleon Bonaparte.

CHAPTER 12

TOUSSAINT was now a benevolent dictator. The constitution set him up as governor of Haiti for life, with the right to select his successor. In the colony his word was law, his power absolute, the only way he felt his people could then be ruled.

Unlike most dictators, the black leader had not established absolute rule for his own glory, and he did not abuse his power. He used it to help his people. Toussaint felt that when Haiti was stronger and more unified, then true democratic rule could be established. For now the blacks had equal rights and equal justice. They were already a long way from slavery.

Toussaint also felt that without France's help and protection, Haiti would flounder economically, and some other colonial power would almost surely try to move in and take over. Determined to maintain the precarious balance between loyalty and independence, hoping against hope that Napoleon would accept Haiti's new political status, Toussaint continued to swear allegiance to France.

A few days after the constitution was proclaimed, the black leader summoned his old friend General Vincent to the government palace. Vincent had always defended Toussaint against criticism, but his loyalty to the black leader had been severely strained by the drawing up of a constitution. He felt the constitution was a slap in Napoleon's face and a fatal mistake.

"I would like you to take the constitution to France and get it approved by Napoleon," Toussaint said to Vincent.

"He'll never approve it now," the French general replied

testily. "It should have been presented for his approval *before* it was proclaimed. If he approves it now, he'll be accepting your right to take such a step. He will be accepting your independence!"

"I see you don't wish to go," said Toussaint, almost sarcastically.

Vincent dreaded the prospect of approaching the First Consul with Toussaint's constitution—a constitution that had already been publicly proclaimed. He was angry at Toussaint for putting him in such a difficult position. "How could you be so ungrateful to France!" he accused the black leader. "France is the only nation that has freed the slaves!"

In the past few days Toussaint had taken much criticism because of his constitution. The mulattoes and whites were especially resentful of his new power, and several French aides had resigned to show their disapproval. The new governor-general of Haiti was feeling tense and on the defensive. When he found his old friend General Vincent taking the same position as all his critics, it was too much.

In a rare fit of temper, Toussaint shouted, "So you want to destroy me, too! Don't think I'm unaware of all the enemies around me! But I'm not at their mercy—and I'm not at your mercy either!"

With that the black leader strode angrily out of the palace and ordered his aides to saddle up his horse, Bel-Argent. Flinging himself onto the stallion, he snapped at the bodyguards who tried to follow him, and rode off alone—through the streets of Le Cap, out onto the open road and up a trail leading into the mountains.

After riding for some time, Toussaint stopped at a small mountain stream and dismounted. He splashed the cool, pure water over his face and then sat down to rest.

Toussaint loved Haiti. He loved the green valleys covered

with swaying seas of sugarcane, the coral beaches and graceful palms, the rugged mountains jutting their peaks proudly into cloudless blue skies and the wild, untamable beauty before him. Haiti was his land, its people were his people. And his land and his people needed him. What were his personal feelings next to the needs of a whole nation? What was his hurt pride next to the horrors that would be inflicted on his people if he abandoned them?

Calmed and refreshed, Toussaint mounted and headed back to his people and the lonely task of being Haiti's first black ruler.

The next day General Vincent agreed to go to France, and two months later the unhappy general stood before Napoleon, a copy of Toussaint's constitution in his hand. The First Consul's reaction was just what Vincent had feared it would be. "This is treason!" Napoleon screamed after reading the contents. "Toussaint has sold out to the British!"

"That is not true, Sire!" protested Vincent. "He has saved the island for you. When George III offered him any title and amount of money if he would hold the island under the British Crown, he refused. He was saving it for France!"

Napoleon was not grateful. He responded by swearing at Vincent, cursing the blacks and calling Toussaint "a revolted Negro."

"I'll strip the epaulette off the shoulder of every Negro in the colony!" the enraged Napoleon shouted.

Vincent still could not believe the First Consul intended to restore slavery in Haiti, despite all the ranting and raving. But Napoleon's little exhibition of racial hatred repelled him, and he began to wonder what fate Napoleon did have in store for Toussaint and his black friends in Haiti.

Toussaint was wondering the same thing, and at the same time preparing for the worst. France was now at peace with all the countries she had been fighting except England. The war with England could end any time now. If Napoleon intended to restore slavery, he would make his move then.

The black leader bought muskets, cannons, gunpowder, swords, saddles and other cavalry equipment from the United States. He built new fortifications, stocked the arsenals and began hiding large stocks of ammunition and supplies in secret places throughout Haiti. All laborers had to report regularly for military training, and Toussaint stepped up training for his regular troops.

So preoccupied was he with these preparations that he no longer had time to go around talking to his people, impressing them with the hard truth—the battle for freedom had not yet been won. The blacks had been warned the French might try to restore slavery, but how could that be true if Toussaint was swearing allegiance to France? And if it were true that France was the enemy, why did they not declare independence? The people were confused, and the only person capable of reassuring them was too preoccupied to do so. Like a busy, benevolent father, he merely told his children to obey and expected they would. After all, it was for their own good.

But the blacks were not children. "Because I say so," even when the person saying it was Toussaint, was not enough of an answer for many of them. Why should they sacrifice some of their liberty now to preserve all of it for the future when they did not see that their future liberty was endangered? Toussaint's failure to clarify to his people what he was doing and why, what they should be doing and why, was to prove a serious oversight. Even more serious was his failure to detect the antagonism of his own generals.

Christophe, Dessalines, Moyse and others of the black generals were now very rich men. They had power, wealth and social position. Unlike Toussaint, they had no desire to soar into the realm of eagles, to risk losing all they had to further the cause of freedom and better the condition of their people. Toussaint's proclaiming of a constitution frightened and infuriated them. It especially angered Moyse and Christophe.

"He has gone too far now," Christophe protested to Moyse. "The constitution is a crime against France. How ridiculous to think we can govern Haiti ourselves. We should be grateful for what we have. I'll revolt against Toussaint rather than support his absurd pretensions."

And Moyse, Toussaint's own nephew, replied, "What does the old fool want? To be king of Haiti? He is arming against France. Where will he get the soldiers to fight? It won't be us, General, who will lead our men against the French."

Moyse was now military commander of the entire Northern Province, the most important post in Haiti next to Toussaint's. A dashing young soldier, he was also the most popular man in the colony after his uncle and a very ambitious person. For some time now he had been harboring thoughts of replacing Toussaint with a younger man—himself.

Moyse began his campaign for power by taking advantage of the discontent among the laborers. "If I had my way, every one of you would have your own farm and be free to work as you pleased. No more plantations—and no more white planters!"

The young commander of the North stirred up so much trouble that production began to lag in his province. When Toussaint reproached him, he told his friends, "No matter what my uncle does, I'm not going to be the executioner of my own color. I'll love the whites when they give me back the eye I lost fighting them. My uncle favors the whites at our expense!"

But while Moyse publicly objected to land being left in the hands of the whites, he was privately leasing out his own plantation to a group of white planters—at a handsome profit to himself. When Toussaint discovered this, he ordered Moyse to cancel the lease. Moyse was now very angry at his uncle.

A few weeks later, as Toussaint and a small contingent of dragoons were heading south toward Port-au-Prince, a breathless courier overtook the party. "General, Moyse's soldiers have aroused the laborers!" the courier cried. "They're massacring whites and looting plantations!"

The black leader stared in disbelief at the courier. "Where's Moyse?"

"I don't know, General. I only know he's not stopping them. And his name is their rallying cry. They're all shouting, 'Long live Moyse!'"

No perfidy of the whites ever upset Toussaint as much as disloyalty from his own people. And Moyse, his own nephew . . . he had trusted Moyse enough to give him the most important command in Haiti.

But Toussaint did not hesitate. After ordering the courier to continue south and alert Dessalines, now in command of the Southern Province, the black leader swung his horse around and headed back to the North, to the rebellious districts.

Stopping only to collect soldiers from the garrisons he passed, Toussaint arrived in the troubled area in record time and scattered the rebels like dust in a storm. Dessalines marched up from the South, and order was restored.

Three hundred whites and almost a thousand blacks had perished. Much property had been destroyed, and all the hostility and hate Toussaint had worked so hard to bury, dug up again.

Moyse was arrested and brought before his uncle. More grim than his aides had ever seen him, Toussaint rebuked his nephew. "You have shamed me and your race. You have endangered the liberty of all your brothers. What is it you want? To get rid of your uncle so you can take his place? Is that it?" demanded Toussaint.

Moyse would not answer. The guards led him away to be tried by the military tribunal.

It was not really a trial. Toussaint was angered and hurt by his nephew's betrayal. He was also troubled by Moyse's popularity. He feared the younger man might try to overthrow him. Until now Moyse had served him well. He was a courageous soldier and an excellent general. Whenever Toussaint thought about a successor, he found himself favoring Moyse. But these were critical times, and the whites, who hated Moyse, were clammering for retribution.

All his life Toussaint had upheld the ideals of justice and fairness. He had decreed that every man in Haiti was entitled to a fair trial. Moyse never got a fair trial. Toussaint's fears of civil war, of Moyse's popularity and of the whites' anger won out over his dedication to justice. To the tribunal the black leader said, "I flatter myself that you will not delay a judgment so necessary to the tranquility of the colony."

The tribunal translated his hint correctly. Moyse was to face the firing squad.

The following day Moyse, his eyes unbandaged, stood bravely before the firing squad. He had stirred up trouble at a most critical time, bringing death to a thousand of his brothers. But he died believing he was right. "Fire, my friends, fire!" he ordered the soldiers. And they obeyed.

Toussaint never recovered from the horror of his own decision. It was to haunt him for the remainder of his life. Yet as many times as he went over it in his mind, he always came up with the same answer, "I had no choice."

Whether Toussaint had a choice or not, he paid dearly for his decision. To the laborers, already unhappy over many of Toussaint's policies, Moyse's execution was an unpardonable crime. Throughout the colony, the voices of dissent grew louder, unsettling a Toussaint whose mind was already in torment and whose soul was beginning to despair. Threatened by the French, criticized and pressured by the whites, betrayed by his nephew and now accused by his own people, he resorted to the oldest weapon of rulers who begin to lose popular support —repression.

Laborers were confined to the plantations more strictly than ever. Soldiers were prohibited from visiting the plantations except to visit their parents. Anyone formenting trouble was sentenced to six months' hard labor. Many of the laborers who had been captured during the uprising were shot.

Little by little the supporters of Moyse were cowed into submission by Toussaint's power. But Toussaint's repressive measures cost him much popularity. Most blacks were still loyal and devoted to him, but the number of those who were not had increased.

In the midst of the black leader's other troubles, news reached Haiti that the war between France and England had ended. Napoleon was free to deal with Haiti and the black who was a threat to his power and his ego.

Toussaint's constitution had angered Napoleon, but he had decided to restore slavery in the colonies long before that. The constitution did, however, serve as an excellent excuse for sending an expedition to Haiti.

Most of Napoleon's generals supported such a move. "The Republic of France has laid down the law to all the rulers of Europe. Will she permit a rebellious black to dictate what she can or cannot do in her own colony?" they asked.

But there were opposing voices too, and many warned the First Consul of the dangers of such an expedition. General Vincent, Toussaint's faithful supporter, pleaded eloquently with Napoleon. "Sire, leave Haiti alone! It is the happiest place in your domain. God meant for Toussaint Louverture to govern. He is the most extraordinary man I've ever met."

Vincent's prophetic warning was lost on Napoleon. But the

high praise for the black who had dared defy him threw Napoleon into a rage.

For his defense of the black leader, Vincent was exiled to the island of Elba. From there he wrote many letters to Toussaint, pleading with him not to irritate Napoleon any further. Even after his exile, the high-principled Vincent could not accept the ugly truth about the First Consul of his country. He could not believe he would restore slavery by force.

Even Josephine, Napoleon's wife, tried to dissuade her husband from sending an expedition to Haiti: "To send an expedition would be a fatal move. It might result in the permanent loss to France of this beautiful colony. Keep Toussaint Louverture—the blacks will not stand for any other leader now. If you strip Toussaint of his power, they will fear a renewal of slavery and fight to their last breath."

Josephine's warning was also lost on Napoleon, who merely sneered at her fears. "I'll have no difficulty trapping Toussaint—or any of those other gilded Africans!"

In response to those who criticized him for being a racist, Napoleon merely shrugged and said, "I am for the whites because I am white. I need no other reason."

But Napoleon had other reasons. The restoration of slavery in Haiti was by now only part of a much grander scheme envisioned by the First Consul.

France had once owned a vast empire in the New World which included Canada and the Louisiana Territory. In 1763, according to the terms of the Peace of Paris, she lost Canada to England and Louisiana to Spain. Since then, except for her colonies in the Caribbean, her possessions in the New World had been insignificant. Napoleon now had an ambitious dream —the restoration of the French colonial empire in the New World. The base of this empire was to be the rich little colony of Haiti.

The First Consul had already taken the first step toward realizing his grand plan—he had bullied Spain into ceding the vast Louisiana Territory back to France. The next step was to invade Haiti. Once Haiti was under control, the French troops would be sent on to Louisiana. Then a mutually beneficial trade would be set up between Louisiana and Haiti to the south, cutting out the United States completely. Supplies would flow up and down the Mississippi River, to and from Haiti, making France's empire in the New World self-supporting and invulnerable.

President Jefferson had few illusions about the fate of the United States if Napoleon built a fortified French empire in the heart of the continent. The young country had only a small army and almost no navy. She was no match for Napoleon's veterans.

The First Consul could not realize his plans for Louisiana until he had Haiti under his thumb. The greatest obstacle to Napoleon's dream for a New World empire was now the black ruler of Haiti. Recognizing this, the United States was all too willing to continue supplying Toussaint with arms and ammunition.

Napoleon had yet another reason for wanting to send troops to Haiti and then on to Louisiana. Many of the men in his army were supporters of the French Revolution who still believed in its democratic ideals. They had fought courageously in the French Revolutionary Wars, thus aiding Napoleon in his climb to power, but they would not be pleased by the next step the First Consul was planning—to make himself Emperor for life. Knowing this, Napoleon said to his Minister of Marine, "There are sixty thousand men whom I want to send as far from France as possible."

The First Consul began to prepare the largest overseas expedition ever to sail from any nation. Headed by his brother-in-law, General Leclerc, it consisted of twenty thousand veteran troops and many of Napoleon's ablest officers. A large fleet of war vessels and transports was assembled to carry the men and supplies. Soon after this contingent sailed, another one of equal strength was to follow.

Shortly before the expedition was to sail, a French colonel who had just returned from Haiti went to Leclerc with some advice. "I know what the planters and colonists say, but don't be lulled by false hopes," he warned Leclerc. "Haiti is a very difficult terrain in which to wage war, and the blacks are not what they were ten years ago."

"Nonsense," replied Leclerc. "When the blacks see my army, they'll drop their arms and run. They'll be only too happy to be pardoned."

"You have been misinformed, General . . . ," said the colonel.

"The French army fears nothing!" shouted Leclerc, storming out of the room.

Across the Atlantic, Toussaint still worked feverishly to prepare his island for the invasion he feared would soon be a reality. The black leader knew Haiti well, and had a good grasp of the problems presented by an all-out invasion. Realizing he would probably have to abandon the coastal towns from the beginning, he began to prepare for the defense of the interior. He made strenuous efforts to increase his regular army, which then numbered about eighteen thousand. And he distributed muskets to nearly one hundred thousand laborers!

While Toussaint prepared, the whites of Haiti gloated. Confident the French were coming to put the black leader down, they dropped the veil of pretense and reverted to their natural arrogance. The whites who sincerely respected and admired Toussaint remained loyal, but they were a minority. Most had only feigned allegiance to get what they wanted. "Your day of reckoning is coming!" they taunted the blacks.

Although Toussaint never fully trusted the whites, he had

been more than fair to them. Such a brazen about-face now, when he most needed them, truly infuriated him. He who had been so free of race prejudice began to feel the beginnings of a bitterness that would one day move him to say, "Don't trust the whites. They'll betray you if they can."

Toussaint was not that disenchanted with the whites yet. But he was very angry, so angry he ordered some of them deported.

A few days after their deportation, a white with whom Toussaint had been very friendly came to him and asked for a passport. "Why do you want to leave, you whom I love and esteem?" Toussaint asked, saddened and disturbed.

"Because I am white and because, although you have kind feelings toward me, you are about to become the wrathful leader of the blacks. Since a few days ago you are no longer the protector of the whites. You have even ordered some of them out of Haiti!"

"Yes," replied Toussaint heatedly, "because they had the impudence and stupidity to rejoice at the news that a French army was coming. As if the arrival of a French army did not spell the doom of the entire colony—their ruin as well as mine!"

If the arrival of the French was to spell the whites' doom, they did not know it. They became increasingly arrogant toward the blacks. When a group of frightened laborers came to Toussaint to seek reassurance, he held up a glass jar filled with black maize and covered on top with a thin layer of white maize. "This represents Haiti," he said. "The whites are on top now. But look . . ." He shook the jar so vigorously the white maize disappeared. "That is what will happen to the whites if the blacks rise in their might!"

Toussaint's agents in France warned him a large expedition was being prepared. Still he did not declare independence.

He just could not seem to accept the barbarous truth about France—that the republic that had proclaimed the Rights of Man and freed the slaves would send soldiers, themselves fighters against tyranny, to restore slavery in Haiti by force.

Until the very last moment, Toussaint never gave up hope that the terrible suffering about to be inflicted on his people could be avoided. He wrote letter after letter to Napoleon, reaffirming his loyalty to France and asking him to help Haiti but allow her to be free.

As the silence on the other side of the Atlantic grew longer and no replies came, Toussaint's messages became more urgent. "Our liberty no longer belongs to France to do with as she pleases. It belongs to us. We shall know how to defend it or perish!"

The blacks were still confused. The French were coming to restore slavery. France was the enemy now. Why didn't Toussaint declare independence?

Why, in the face of aggression, Toussaint hesitated to declare independence, we may never know. But when the first French soldier stepped ashore, the French flag was still flying over Haiti.

CHAPTER 13

ON the afternoon of January 29, 1802, the blue waters of Samana Bay looked cool and inviting to the sentry sweating under the brilliant Santo Domingo sun. As he walked back and forth along the deserted beach, he would stop now and then, and, shading his eyes with his hand, gaze out toward the horizon. He saw nothing but the cloudless sky and peaceful waters of the bay.

On a cliff high above the bay, a man in a general's uniform, seated on a white stallion, also peered intensely out over the water. At this vantage point on the cliff, Toussaint saw the first tiny sail appear in the distance, then a second sail and a third . . . As the sails continued to appear, the black leader let out a cry of dismay, "We are doomed! All France has come to overwhelm us!"

But Toussaint's panic was brief. "I am a soldier and afraid of no man," he reminded himself and his aides. "I fear only God. If I must die, it shall be as a soldier of honor with no self-reproach."

With that rebuke to himself, he began the hard ride back to French Haiti and the city of Le Cap, where the main fleet under Leclerc himself was to land.

The black leader had not expected the French fleet to arrive so soon. When British sources warned him the ships were only a few hours away, Toussaint was far from Le Cap. Having done all he could to prepare French Haiti for the invasion, he had hurried to Santo Domingo to organize the Spanish colony's defense, leaving General Christophe in charge of Le Cap. Christophe had been ordered to allow no French ship to land without Toussaint's permission. Now Toussaint had to leave the defense of Santo Domingo in his brother's hands and rush back to Le Cap, where he was most needed.

The French expedition consisted of the first half of the forty thousand veteran troops Napoleon was sending, as well as some of Napoleon's ablest officers. They were among the best France had to offer, and Napoleon had ordered them to do their job in two months. Most of the officers considered the expedition a lark, and were amused at being given so much time to put down the blacks. "All we have to do is land, and the blacks will lay down their arms. What do we need two months for?" they asked each other.

Also on board Leclerc's flagship was Pauline, his beautiful wife and Napoleon's favorite sister. Small and fair, with blue eyes and flaxen hair, she was much like the Creole ladies—with that special air of languor that accompanies soft living and a spiritless soul. With her she brought an elegant wardrobe and all the makings of a French court—musicians, artists, actors, dancers. If she had to reside in "barbaric" Haiti for two long months while slavery was being restored, at least she was going to have a good time.

Phase one of Napoleon's plan for the expedition might best be entitled "Deceit." Leclerc was to issue a proclamation signed by the First Consul assuring the blacks the rumors they had heard were false.

"Citizens! If anyone tells you the French army is here to take away your liberty, answer them, 'The Republic has given us liberty. The Republic will not permit it to be taken from us.' Rally around General Leclerc. He brings you peace and plenty. Those who oppose him are traitors to their country."

The proclamation also promised that Toussaint and his generals would be allowed to remain in their posts. If the blacks refused to swallow all those lies and cooperate, then the French were to move to the next two phases of the plan, capturing all the coastal towns and, finally, moving into the interior to take Toussaint himself. The fourth phase was, of course, the restoration of slavery.

The blacks were hardly the only victims of Napoleon's deceit in this expedition. The First Consul had convinced his soldiers that Toussaint was a tyrant who had betrayed his people and the democratic ideals of the Revolution by selling out to royalist England. To prevent their discovering the truth, Napoleon had given orders to his officers that any soldier who discussed the rights of the blacks should be sent back to France.

The blacks and the French soldiers were not the only targets of Napoleon's deceit. Even the Americans were to be duped. The United States now had many investments in Haiti, and carried on a brisk trade with the colony. Before the expedition sailed, the Americans were reassured by the French that their interests in Haiti would be protected and that there would be no interference in trade. But Napoleon's secret plans were to restore the French monopoly.

The size of the expedition being sent to Haiti did not reassure the Americans. They were now convinced that the First Consul intended to carry out his scheme for a New World empire.

As Toussaint was racing toward Le Cap, the main fleet under General Leclerc dropped anchor just beyond the reefs of Le Cap's harbor. Christophe ordered the harbormaster to row out to the fleet and board the flagship.

Unhappily eyeing the awesome fleet ahead, the harbormaster did as he was told, and soon reached the ship. A rope ladder was thrown over the side, and he climbed aboard. "I have a message for General Leclerc," he announced, ignoring the curious and amused stares of the smartly uniformed whites who surrounded him.

"I am General Leclerc. What is the message?"

The harbormaster turned to see a handsome but somewhat effeminate-looking man in his late twenties, with thick, dark hair and sideburns. He was dressed in full general's uniform.

"The governor-general is in the Spanish part of the island. Without his permission, you cannot land," said the harbormaster to Leclerc.

Delighted with this news, Leclerc demanded, "Who is in command of Le Cap?"

"General Christophe."

"Tell General Christophe my aide-de-camp will come ashore in an hour with my reply."

An hour later several of Christophe's officers, dressed in simple but handsome uniforms, met Lebrun, Leclerc's aide-de-camp, at the quay. They gave him a horse and escorted him to the government palace.

Hundreds of people crowded the street along the harbor to look with awe at the formidable French fleet. As Lebrun rode by, he was struck by the very different expressions on their faces—the blacks looked at him with anger and resentment; some of the mulattoes regarded him with hostility, while others seemed either pleased or indifferent; the whites could barely disguise their glee.

The heat was so intolerable Lebrun found it somewhat difficult just to breathe. Glancing occasionally at the black officers escorting him, he wondered how they remained so cool and composed.

The city of Le Cap also made him wonder. He had been led to believe that under the blacks the "Paris of the Antilles" had fallen into decay. Yet he could see no evidence of that. In fact, he saw many signs of prosperity.

As they approached the government palace, the French aide saw ahead an imposing white edifice surrounded by well-kept gardens. He was ushered inside through the white marble halls into a tastefully furnished room hung with gold brocade. A minute later Christophe entered. "I am General Christophe. What is the reply you bring?"

Stepping toward Christophe and lowering his voice, Lebrun said, "If you will allow the French army to land, General Leclerc will shower you with honors and favors."

"Never!" shouted Christophe angrily. "I have sworn to maintain liberty at any cost! You will remain here while I dictate an answer to General Leclerc."

Christophe withdrew from the room, leaving Lebrun alone. From the windows the French aide could see his ships waiting just beyond the dangerous reefs that enveloped the harbor. As the hours passed and the indigo sky became streaked with the exotic colors of a tropical sunset, Lebrun wondered if he was a prisoner.

Just as darkness fell, two servants entered the room, carrying trays of food. Without a word they pulled the drapes, lit the candles and set a small table with a white lace cloth, heavy silver goblets and silver utensils.

As he ate the meal they laid before him, Lebrun could not help but marvel at the excellent food. It compared with the finest he had ever had in Paris! When he had completed his meal, Lebrun was given Christophe's reply and escorted back to the waterfront.

Leclerc was annoyed. He had felt certain Christophe would snatch at any promise of power and glory he dangled before him. Now his task would be a little more difficult.

About midnight a boat was lowered and Lebrun again rowed ashore, this time with a formal written message from Leclerc to Christophe that ended: "Thousands of French troops are at this moment landing at coastal cities all over Haiti. I warn you that if you have not turned over the city's forts to me by daybreak tomorrow, fifteen thousand soldiers will be disembarked. I hold you responsible for what may happen."

The ultimatum, intended to intimidate Christophe, only infuriated him. Lebrun did not have to wait long this time for Christophe's angry reply.

"If you use force to land, I will resist. If you succeed in landing, you will set foot in a city reduced to ashes. Even on those ashes I will continue to fight you. As for those troops you say are ready to land, I consider them a house of cards that will be scattered by the wind."

As soon as Lebrun had left, Christophe commanded his officers, "Evacuate the population immediately!"

That night, soldiers went from door to door, warning the people of Le Cap to leave the city. Soon rich and poor, black, white and mulatto—all but the soldiers—had headed for safety in the hills.

At daybreak the wind changed, and Leclerc, fearing the dangerous reefs, made no move. All day the mulatto commander of Fort Picolet, which guarded the harbor, kept watch. His orders from Christophe were, "As soon as one ship moves through the channel into the harbor, fire the cannon to warn us."

That night, as the oil lamps of the French ships gleamed softly in the distance, a cluster of lights detached itself from the main fleet and headed noiselessly toward the channel. The commander of Fort Picolet saw the black frigate sail through the reefs into the harbor.

"Fire!" he shouted at his men.

The sound of the cannon's boom bounded off the mountains and rumbled through the valley. All over Le Cap black and mulatto soldiers lit their torches and rushed into the streets.

Christophe leaped onto his horse and galloped toward his home, one of the city's most stately mansions. His family and servants had already fled, and the house was deserted. With a lighted torch he rushed from room to room, setting fire to the luxurious drapes, the beautiful and valuable Gobelin tapestry, lace tablecloths, anything that would catch fire quickly.

In a few minutes all the treasures and royal splendor that had been such a source of pride to Christophe and his family were enveloped in flames. Fleeing the inferno, he remounted his horse and galloped through the streets, shouting commands.

The "Paris of the Antilles" was again in flames—the customhouse, the theater, the church, the government palace, all the little shops and the pink, white and yellow houses. Burning molasses poured from the warehouses and ran through the streets like lava.

From the hills above, the refugees saw their city burn. For many it was not the first time they had lost their homes to fire. As they watched, some weeping, some praying, a deafening explosion in the city shook the earth on which they stood. The arsenal of Le Cap had blown up.

The explosion was followed by a long, low rumble. The people in the hills looked up. In the eerie light of the city's fire, they saw huge boulders, loosened by the shock of the explosion, hurtling down the side of the mountain above them.

People screamed, women threw themselves over their children, men shouted commands—all in vain. There was neither shelter nor time, and many were crushed.

The fire in the city raged all night. The following morning, the French landed.

When Pauline set her dainty foot onshore, her little French shoe was immediately blackened with ashes. Her playground-to-be was a burned-out shell. Only about sixty of Le Cap's two thousand houses still stood, and their once-lovely pastel walls were now charred and crumbling, their delicate balcony railings twisted and grotesque.

Lifting her skirt gingerly, Pauline stepped off the dock into the street. The city smelled of fire and death, and the air, still filled with smoke and cinders, made her eyes water. She took a step, and her little shoes stuck to the pavement. Looking down she saw the streets were covered with sticky, burned molasses.

Bursting into sobs, she fled back to the boat and demanded to be rowed out to the flagship. Leclerc allowed her to leave, and Pauline lived on board ship until a beautiful mansion was prepared for her in the hills above Le Cap.

About the same moment Pauline stepped ashore, Toussaint reached the hills above Le Cap. He had been riding hard for several days without sleep, living on bananas and water. Of the men who left Santo Domingo with him, only two had been able to keep up. The rest came straggling in the following day, and a few the day after.

A messenger had warned Toussaint of Leclerc's arrival. The second message never reached him, but as soon as Toussaint saw the red glow in the sky above Le Cap, he knew. Now he stood looking down through the smoke-clogged valley at the devastated city—his city, the city he had worked so hard to rebuild, the city he loved. In the harbor he saw the French fleet and dozens of small boats discharging men on his shore. Soldiers in white uniforms and shiny boots were marching crisply through the deserted, burned-out streets.

Christophe, who had fled to the hills with his men after setting fire to the city, came galloping up to Toussaint and saluted.

Turning toward him, Toussaint spoke with difficulty. "Who ordered the city fired?"

"I did, General," replied Christophe.

"Why didn't you make some military arrangements to defend the city until I arrived?" the black leader demanded.

"My duty and the circumstances forced me to do it," replied Christophe.

Toussaint knew he was right. He would have given the order himself. Christophe was not to blame. France, not Christophe, had destroyed his beautiful city.

The two generals then withdrew to the temporary headquarters Christophe had set up in the hills to discuss strategy.

For many months before the French arrived, Toussaint had been laying plans for an ingenious mode of defense. He had less than twenty thousand regular troops, too few to stretch along the coast for an effective defense, and his coastal batteries were no match for the big guns of the French warships. Therefore, he had decided that just before the French landed he would take his army into the interior, leaving only a small garrison in each major coastal town. When the French tried to land in a town, the garrison would set fire to it and retreat into the interior, rousing the black laborers as they went. After the forces had rendezvoused, Toussaint would swing back and recapture the coastal towns one by one.

It was a brilliant plan and proof of Toussaint's military genius. That it would have succeeded, even Pamphile de Lacroix, chief-of-staff of Napoleon's expedition, admitted. But after months of planning and only a short time before the French landed, Toussaint's generals had opposed the plan. Ambitious for personal glory and more romantic than Toussaint about their own strength, they decided they wanted to hold their ground and resist French landings in their territories. They did not want to give up their personal commands, retreat and then all unite under Toussaint.

Too late Christophe recognized their mistake, admitting to General de Lacroix many months later, "If we had retreated and alarmed the laborers instead of fighting, you wouldn't have gotten the best of us. Toussaint kept saying it and saying it, but we wouldn't listen. We had arms. It hurt our pride not to use them. This was our undoing."

There was a time when Toussaint's generals would have obeyed any plan he came up with, and without hesitation. But Toussaint had lost the strong hold he once had on his generals, and his execution of Moyse had made them angry and somewhat distrustful. Faced with resistance from his officers, the black leader had been forced to scatter his army along the coast.

Now what he had feared was happening. While Toussaint was at Christophe's camp, messengers kept arriving, bringing news of other French landings in major coastal cities. The garrison at Port-au-Prince was commanded by the white general Agé, upon whom Toussaint had showered many favors. Agé had surrendered willingly to his fellow whites. Many mulatto officers, seeing the flag of the French Republic, threw down their arms shouting, "Long live France! Long live our brothers!"

In all instances, the blacks were faced with greater numbers and superior arms. They put up a brave and stubborn resistance, but in one coastal town after another they were forced to retreat, leaving the town in French hands.

The French General Rochambeau took Fort Dauphin and ordered all prisoners shot. When Toussaint heard this piece of news, he warned the French, "I will fight to the last to avenge the death of those brave men, to preserve liberty and to restore peace and order in Haiti!"

The burning of Le Cap and the execution of the blacks by Rochambeau had put Toussaint in a rage. With Christophe, he sat down to map out new strategy. "We will wait for the rainy season, which will deliver us from our enemies," Toussaint began. "Until then, fire and destruction remain our only course of action. All generals in charge of coastal towns will set fire to their town and retreat if they find they cannot defend it. The land that has been bathed with our sweat and blood must not yield a crumb of food to our enemy!"

Christophe agreed vigorously. No longer did he believe the generals should resist the French landings and not retreat. He had seen the strength of the French forces.

"Raid the roads!" Toussaint commanded Christophe, his voice rising in anger. "Throw the bodies of dead horses into the wells and springs. Burn and destroy the buildings, crops, livestock, anything the French can use. Those who have come to enslave us will find here the image of hell they so richly deserve!"

Toussaint's orders were carried out. Dessalines, following Christophe's example, set fire to his own mansion at St.-Marc. At Port-de-Paix, the French ordered a young black general to surrender the town. The general replied by setting fire to the town and withdrawing, killing two hundred of the French soldiers who tried to stop his men.

Soon the French controlled most of the coast. The whites of Santo Domingo, quickly forgetting all the black ruler had done for their colony, welcomed their fellow whites with open arms and surrendered to the French. Paul Louverture, still in command of the colony, sent an urgent message to Toussaint. But it was intercepted, and he was forced to flee, leaving the Spanish colony to the French.

The second phase of Napoleon's plan, the capture of strategic coastal towns, had been carried out. Leclerc now began laying plans for phase three, the capture of Toussaint, who had set up temporary headquarters at Gonaïves, a town near the northwest coast.

Five French armies prepared for the attack to capture one man—the man a colonist had bragged he could take with sixty grenadiers.

CHAPTER 14

LECLERC intended to capture Toussaint at any cost, but if he could do it without force, so much the better. Before ordering the attack, he decided to employ the most shameful weapon of deceit Napoleon had prepared—Toussaint's sons.

Toussaint had become increasingly concerned about the fate of his son and stepson, who were still in school in Paris. His letters to Napoleon requesting their return had been unanswered, along with all his other letters.

Isaac, now about sixteen, and Toussaint's stepson, Placide, now about twenty-one, were very well treated in Paris. One day, shortly before the expedition to Haiti sailed, Napoleon ordered the two young men brought to him.

After greeting them cordially, he said, "Your father is a great man. He has rendered an important service to France. I am sending you both to Haiti to see him. Tell him that I, First Consul of France, promise him protection, honor and glory. Do not let anyone tell you that France is going to wage war in Haiti. The army is going there not to defeat the forces of your country but to strengthen them."

Napoleon then presented Toussaint's sons with impressive French uniforms and full armor, and allowed them to dine with him. Too young to possess their father's worldly astuteness, they were completely taken in by Napoleon. They left for Haiti with the expedition, convinced of the First Consul's sincerity.

When they witnessed the burning of Le Cap, however, they naturally began to suspect Napoleon's intentions. Leclerc used lies to calm their fears and persuaded them to take a letter from Napoleon to Toussaint and to use their influence with their father to bring about peace.

Two days later Isaac and Placide arrived with their tutor at Ennery and were greeted with tears by their mother, who had not seen them in about five years. Shortly before midnight Toussaint's heavily guarded carriage pulled up in front of the plantation house. Isaac and Placide rushed to greet their father, and Toussaint, stern soldier that he was, wept as he embraced them.

When they had all retired to the drawing room, Isaac presented his father with a gold-enameled box fastened with a tricolor silken cord and Napoleon's official seal. Toussaint opened the box and found the first and only letter the First Consul had ever deigned to write him.

Addressing Toussaint as one of France's "most illustrious

citizens," Napoleon praised him for his services to Haiti and France—and then proceeded to insult him:

"What is it that you want? Liberty for the blacks? You know very well that wherever the French have gone they have brought liberty to people who had none. Or perhaps you desire personal honors and fortune? If that is so, can you doubt that you will receive them in full measure after the services you have rendered?"

After insulting Toussaint by insinuating he was seeking personal glory, the First Consul assured him France's intentions were peaceful and demanded that Toussaint recognize Leclerc's authority.

Angered by the letter, Toussaint turned to the tutor, Abbé Coisnon, and said, "One talks to me of peace. The other wages war on me! If Napoleon really wants peace, then let Leclerc cease his aggressions. I am willing to enter into negotiations, but not until he ceases his hostilities."

Abbé Coisnon was a sincere man who believed Napoleon and Leclerc were also sincere men. "Go to Le Cap and confer with Leclerc," he pleaded.

"No," replied Toussaint, shaking his head. "It's too late for that. The war is in full swing. My soldiers' blood is up, and they will win or die. If General Leclerc really wants peace, you can tell him to cease his hostilities now and give us back our colony. Only that will save Haiti from total destruction."

Toussaint's sons had been silent throughout the conversation. Now they too joined Abbé Coisnon in pleading with their father to go see Leclerc.

Turning to Isaac and Placide, Toussaint spoke gently: "I do not blame you for feeling attached to France. If you wish to do so, you are free to go and serve that country. But I cannot compromise the future of my people."

Tearfully, his sons begged him to lay down his arms and

make peace with Leclerc. Shaking his head again, Toussaint said, "I have made my choice, and you must do the same. You must choose between Haiti and France. No matter which way you choose, I will always love you."

Sadly Isaac said, "I cannot bear arms against France," and, turning his back on his father, walked out of the room.

Placide walked up to Toussaint, and said softly, "I will stay with you, Father. I'm ready to fight any attempt to restore slavery. I renounce France."

Embracing his stepson, Toussaint said, "You will be my aide-de-camp."

Placide smiled proudly, ignoring Abbé Coisnon, who clucked his disapproval.

Isaac remained at Ennery with his mother and younger brother, and Toussaint and Placide left for Gonaïves. Abbé Coisnon returned, alone and sad, to Le Cap, where he advised Leclerc of Toussaint's refusal.

Leclerc promptly issued a proclamation declaring Toussaint, Christophe and Dessalines rebels and outlaws. In February, almost three weeks after the expedition had landed, five French armies began to march toward Gonaïves.

A few days after Toussaint returned to his headquarters, an aide burst into his workroom. "General, the French are coming! Five armies are headed this way!"

Christophe had been driven farther and farther inland, and the French were advancing on Gonaïves from four different directions. They had already reached Ennery.

"And my family?" Toussaint asked the aide.

"They have fled into the mountains, General." Hesitating, the aide said softly, "We do not know exactly where they are, but . . . your youngest son got separated from his mother and is now a prisoner of the French."

"Saint-Jean?" Toussaint asked.

"Yes, General."

Toussaint asked no more questions. Forcing his personal problems out of his mind, he turned to the most urgent task at hand—the French.

Toussaint had under his direct personal command about three thousand regular troops—grenadiers of the guard, dragoons and infantrymen—and some twenty-four hundred armed laborers. The black leader sent off reinforcements to Christophe, and ordered the mulatto general Vernet to fight a delaying action at Gonaïves. Then he himself headed off at the head of fifteen hundred grenadiers and sixty dragoons to meet General Rochambeau, who had under his command four thousand of Napoleon's crack troops.

Before leaving on this mission, Toussaint addressed his men:

"You are going out to fight against men who have neither faith, law nor religion. Because you will not be their slaves, they call you 'rebels.' For nearly three centuries you were subjected to abject servitude, tortures and all kinds of cruelties. Then you saw this land of slavery purified by fire and made more beautiful than ever under freedom. Now the mother country, seduced by the First Consul, has become a cruel stepmother. It is not for liberty or the motherland that the French make war on us. It is only to satisfy the ambition of Napoleon Bonaparte! But they will not succeed. Those whom our sword fails to strike down will be slain by our harsh and avenging climate. Their bones will be scattered among these mountains and bleached by the waves of the sea. Never more will they see their native land. Haiti will be their tomb, and over their graves liberty will reign!"

Toussaint made his stand at Ravine-à-Couleuvres, known as "Snake Gully," through which Rochambeau would have to pass. A wild place filled with treacherous gorges and prickly cactus, it was well suited to the kind of guerrilla warfare in which the blacks excelled.

Six hundred grenadiers were stationed on top of the highest plateaus overlooking the gully, while the rest of Toussaint's men lay flat on the ground or behind rocks. About fifteen hundred laborers, armed with axes and hatchets, hid in the surrounding woods. They were to harry the enemy's flanks, but not join battle until Toussaint gave the word.

At dawn the first of the French troops were sighted. The blacks made neither a sound nor a movement. They waited, guns in hand, for Toussaint's order. The French soldiers, suspecting nothing, headed toward the gully.

As they entered, Toussaint gave the order to fire. A torrent of bullets tore into the enemy. The black general dismounted from his horse and, sword in hand, charged into the French ranks at the head of his grenadiers.

General Rochambeau also dismounted and fought side by side with his soldiers. For several hours Snake Gully was filled with the horrible sights and sounds of swords, bayonets, blood, terror and death.

Although greatly outnumbered, the blacks had the upper hand right from the start. The French, taken by surprise, fought frantically at first, but by noon Toussaint noticed that some of the fury had gone out of their fighting. He gave the laborers the signal. Wild cries echoed through the gully, and fifteen hundred blacks waving axes and hatchets poured out of the woods and swarmed over the French.

This second unexpected and completely unconventional attack was too much for Napoleon's veterans. Already exhausted from hours of hand-to-hand combat with blacks who fought with singular skill and ferocity, the French began throwing down their bayonets and surrendering. Above the sounds of battle, General Rochambeau's voice could be heard shouting to his men, "These are only slaves you're fighting. They're only slaves! Have you come thousands of miles to be beaten by rebellious slaves?"

But finally Rochambeau was forced to order a retreat, and the French poured back out of the gully, leaving hundreds of prisoners behind.

Toussaint had broken the circle closing in on him. With his men and the French prisoners, he headed for safety in the Cahos Mountains, where he had concealed his main store of arms and ammunition.

When Leclerc learned of Toussaint's victory over Rochambeau, he headed his army inland in pursuit of the black leader.

The entrance to the Cahos Mountains was commanded by Crête-à-Pierrot, a key fortress. Toussaint knew if he stationed a strong garrison there, the fort would be almost impregnable, and Leclerc would have to concentrate all his energy on taking it. Otherwise, the blacks would be in an excellent position to bar his way into the interior and to threaten French communications. While Leclerc was concentrating on taking the fortress, Toussaint and Christophe would be free to operate behind the French lines, capturing supplies, cutting communications and generally harassing the enemy until the rainy season arrived.

The black general stationed twelve hundred men at Crête-à-Pierrot under the command of Dessalines. As soon as Leclerc learned of this maneuver, he realized what Toussaint was up to. But, as in the game of chess, Toussaint had made the critical move. Leclerc had no choice but to expose other strategic points while he concentrated on the most important one, Crête-à-Pierrot.

As the sun rose one clear morning in March, Dessalines, naked to the waist, was strolling the ramparts of the fort. In the distance below he saw the first contingent of the magnificent

French army enter the plain. Soon the weapons of twelve thousand men were gleaming in the early sunlight.

Dessalines immediately summoned the entire garrison of twelve hundred men before him. "We will be attacked this morning. I want only brave men here. Those who are content to be slaves may leave. Those who wish to die free, rally round me now!"

With shouts and clenched fists, the garrison proclaimed their preference for death over slavery. Grabbing a burning torch and holding it over a keg of gunpowder, Dessalines cried, "If the French manage to set foot in this fort, I'll blow us all to glory! We'll die, but we'll all be free!"

So greatly outnumbered were they, the blacks had to rely solely on their wits and courage. Their first move was a masterful trick which fooled the French completely.

Dessalines ordered his men to clear away the trees from the steep slope of the ravine outside the fort. Then he had them dig several rows of ditches a few feet deep, all within gunshot distance of the fort. When this work was completed, Dessalines set out from the fort at the head of a small detachment of his best soldiers. The men hid in the woods some distance from the fort, relaxing and chatting.

After several hours had gone by, the front line of French soldiers came into sight, marching stiffly and confidently—straight toward the blacks. The blacks leaped from their hiding places, shrieking loudly, and fled rapidly in the direction of the fort. The French took up the pursuit and, guns drawn, rushed headlong toward the fort.

When the French soldiers came into the fort's firing range, the blacks they were pursuing suddenly disappeared. The earth seemed to have swallowed them up, leaving the French exposed. Dessalines gave the command, and the fort opened fire. Bullets ripped into the French line, taking a heavy toll.

Black Patriot and Martyr

As the French began to retreat, the blacks they had been pursuing appeared out of nowhere and began to pursue the fleeing soldiers. The French turned back and, bayonets drawn, again charged after the blacks. And again, as they drew near the fort, the blacks disappeared and the fort opened fire.

When the second exchange ended, eight hundred French soldiers lay dead or wounded. Two French generals were seriously wounded. The pursued blacks, unscathed by bullets, climbed out of the trenches into which they had twice leaped, fooling the French both times at great cost to the enemy.

It would not be the last time the blacks outwitted Napoleon's veterans with their unconventional guerrilla-warfare tactics. But there were still over eleven thousand French soldiers out there and only twelve hundred blacks. A lot of cleverness was needed to change that.

Under cover of darkness, Dessalines slipped out of the fort to find reinforcements and harass the enemy from the rear. Before he left, he made everyone swear they would not surrender. The mulatto general Lamartinière was left in charge of the fort. Fighting right alongside of him was his young mulatto wife.

The French artillery began to pound the fort. The bombardment went on, day and night, night and day. But each time the French launched an assault, they encountered a spirited defense and lost many men.

Inside the fort, five hundred blacks lay dead or wounded. The survivors were running short of provisions and water. Without water, the intense heat became almost insufferable. Hoping to soothe their burning throats by stimulating a flow of saliva, the men began chewing on lead bullets. The wounded begged for poison so their suffering would not demoralize the others. Still, the red flag signifying "no quarter" flew defiantly above the fort.

At night, the French soldiers camped in the plain could hear the strains of the *Marseillaise, Ça Ira* and other French revolutionary songs coming from the fort. Moved by the familiar strains, they began to speculate on the hideous truth. Was Napoleon really intending to restore slavery? Were they, soldiers of liberty and equality, being used for such a monstrous purpose? But their officers vehemently denied any such intent, and the confused soldiers went on fighting and dying to defeat the enemy who had "sold out" to the royalists—an enemy whose true aims they would have warmly embraced had they not been so treacherously deceived.

As the days went by, a frustrated Leclerc reported to Napoleon, "The blacks die, but they do not surrender."

One day two blacks slipped through the French army surrounding the fort with a message from Dessalines. "There are no reinforcements. Evacuate the fort."

About six hundred men, half of the original garrison, had managed somehow to survive the deadly French bombardments and assaults. Soldiers still completely surrounded the fort. How, the mulatto commander wondered, could he possibly get six hundred men past thousands of French soldiers?

On the first moonless night Lamartinière decided to take the last chance his men had. While the armies of General Leclerc and General de Lacroix bombarded the fort, General Rochambeau and his men were camped in the ravine below the fort. The soldiers were sleeping peacefully when the night silence was rudely broken by the sounds of wild shouts and howls, and an army of demons fell on them. Six hundred blacks, making enough noise for six thousand, burst through the camp, scattering the startled soldiers in all directions. Rochambeau himself fled into the woods in his pajamas.

The retreat, one of the most amazing in history, was a success.

As Toussaint had hoped, the French paid a very high price to take Crête-à-Pierrot. They lost about two thousand men and much precious time. So ashamed was Leclerc that he lied about his losses to Napoleon, and forbade his officers to tell the truth.

The victory in Snake Gully and the defense of Crête-à-Pierrot did wonders for restoring the blacks' morale. For the first time they began to feel they were equal to the French soldiers, despite the latter's superior numbers and impressive arms.

While the courageous blacks and mulattoes were defending Crête-à-Pierrot, Toussaint had sped north, calling up the black laborers as he went. Thousands of laborers joined Toussaint, and his army gave the French no rest, harassing them night and day, cutting off their communications and supplies and causing serious damage to the soldiers' morale.

Toussaint began engaging the French in short skirmishes, breaking off action as soon as he had inflicted enough damage. Sometimes he would suddenly loom out of the dark, slash into the enemy and disappear before the French had even spotted his scarlet plume, only to reappear a few miles away to ambush another regiment. In this way he kept the French in a constant state of tension.

The blacks used every imaginable kind of guerrilla tactic to harry the French. They climbed steep cliffs, rolled enormous rocks to the edge of the precipice, and pushed them down on the French when they marched below. They dug huge pits and covered them with branches so the mounted soldiers would fall in with their horses. They blockaded strategic roads with fallen trees and thorny bushes.

As the French struggled with these obstacles, invisible blacks shot at them from atop cliffs, from the branches of trees or from behind rocks and shrubs. Sometimes a French regiment marching through the mountains lost half its men without ever spotting the enemy. Leclerc complained to Napoleon, "It is like fighting Arabs. As soon as we pass, the black forces occupy the woods and cut off our communications."

To make matters worse for the French, Toussaint had discovered that, unlike himself, most men needed regular sleep. A tired, nervous soldier was not a good fighter.

Toussaint issued orders to harass the French while they slept. Everywhere the blacks launched small-scale surprise attacks that were broken off as soon as the French engaged in combat. Being thoroughly familiar with the terrain, they easily lost the French soldiers who tried to pursue them. The next night the blacks would be back, and again they would break off as soon as the French began to fight. The following night the French waited and waited, but the blacks didn't come. So nervous were they waiting for the attack that sleep was out of the question.

Sometimes the blacks would not attack, but merely let the French know they were nearby. Late one night French scouts heard loud whispers near their camp. "Platoon, halt! To the right, dress!"

This was repeated twenty times in twenty different places along an extended line. The scouts warned the camp to prepare for an attack by a large force, and all night the soldiers were on the alert. In the morning the French discovered they had been fooled by about one hundred laborers. Their exasperated general commented, "If we pay too much attention to these ruses, it destroys the men's morale. If we neglect them, we could become victims of a surprise attack."

Toussaint recaptured several towns from the French. One day, as he was returning to Marmelade, where he had set up temporary headquarters, Toussaint noticed the sky had turned gray and he heard a rumble of thunder in the distance. As he rode, the sky went from gray to black, and in another moment a torrent of rain came down. The dry dust beneath his horse's hoofs quickly became thick black mud. The rainy season had begun.

The two months Napoleon had allocated for subduing the blacks had passed, and Leclerc's situation was not good. By the end of April he had lost five thousand men in battle, and thousands more had been hospitalized with injuries or tropical diseases. To Napoleon he sent a dreary report. "The rainy season has arrived. My troops are exhausted with fatigue and sickness. I can no longer hope to take Haiti without reinforcements."

Fearing Napoleon's anger at such a disastrous turn of events, Leclerc added to his letter, "France must not worry about the money it is spending to ensure its possession of the finest colony in the world. It is here at this moment that the question of whether France will preserve any colonies in the West Indies is being decided."

Napoleon did not have to be reminded of the importance of Haiti to the white world and the colonial powers. But such unexpected bungling threw him into a rage.

While the French fell in battle or succumbed to the dread yellow fever to which the blacks were immune, Toussaint's position grew stronger every day. No longer did the French officers adopt a cocky attitude toward Toussaint and his army. Many openly admired the military prowess of the black general and his soldiers.

Even General de Lacroix gave the blacks credit. Describing a recent encounter to Leclerc, he said, "We struck blow after blow, but the blacks seemed only to multiply after each one. The name Toussaint Louverture is on everybody's lips!"

Toussaint of Haiti

Toussaint's fortunes were on the rise again. With the rainy season on his side, the French army awaited his next move with fear and dread.

CHAPTER 15

TOUSSAINT began to plan a massive attack that would have spelled death to what remained of the French army. But he did not go through with it. Instead, he decided, now, at the peak of his power, to come to terms with the French.

The reasons for Toussaint's decision were probably as complex and obscure as his own character. Historians to this day are still debating about his motivation. Some say he was actually planning a very clever trap to completely destroy the French. Others say he was just helping France save face. Toussaint knew that such a great colonial power would be very unwilling to admit defeat by the blacks of Haiti. The war would grind on and on, with thousands more blacks and Frenchmen being killed.

What is certain is that Toussaint hated war and preferred diplomacy to slaughter. If he could do anything to avoid violence, bloodshed and death, he did it. By coming to terms at the height of his power, he felt he could win most of what he would gain by killing every last Frenchman in Haiti. Had the French leaders been men of high moral principles, as was Toussaint himself, his assessment might have been correct. But the black leader was dealing with Napoleon Bonaparte and his equally ruthless supporters.

General Leclerc was also anxious to end the war. His men were exhausted and demoralized by the most difficult war they had ever known. Not knowing Toussaint planned to negotiate, he decided to try bribing Toussaint's chief officers into surrendering.

The first general whom Leclerc approached was Christophe. It was a shrewd choice. An outstanding general and a good man in many ways, Christophe had serious weaknesses. Before Napoleon's expedition landed, he had got along well with the whites, often surprising the French with his worldliness and sophistication. He was a man who enjoyed his worldly comforts, and now, in his late thirties, he was sick of fighting. "I'm tired of living in the woods like a bandit!" he complained openly.

General Leclerc sent Christophe a letter, promising to shower him with honors and rewards if he would lay down his arms. Christophe was tempted, but then Leclerc wrecked everything by sending a second letter in which he suggested that Christophe capture Toussaint.

Insulted by this vile proposal, Christophe took Leclerc's letters to Toussaint himself. The black leader then made the first of a series of mistakes. He instructed Christophe to continue negotiating with Leclerc to see what he would propose next. When the French general finally suggested a meeting with Christophe, Toussaint instructed him to go. "But be very circumspect. Do not commit yourself to anything. Tell Leclerc you will think over whatever he proposes. Then report back to me."

Leclerc and Christophe met in Le Cap. The French general greeted the black officer with an effusive display of respect and courtesy. By the end of the interview Christophe, who only a few days before had been so shocked at the thought of betraying his chief, had been cajoled into surrendering his entire army to Leclerc.

It was a shattering blow to Toussaint, the blacks and the cause of the rebellion. But Toussaint was not without blame.

He should never have trusted another man to deal with a polished contriver like Leclerc.

When word of Christophe's betrayal got out, the blacks were very angry. Many of the soldiers and officers under his command deserted and went over to Toussaint, rather than join the French. But the black leader was still in a very difficult position.

Now that he had Christophe, Leclerc figured he was in a better position to get Toussaint to negotiate. He sent the black leader a conciliatory note. "It will be a happy day for me when you come to an agreement with us and submit to the Republic."

Toussaint knew his negotiating power had been greatly undermined by Christophe's defection. He also knew that as the rainy season progressed, the yellow fever would continue to reduce the French army. The weaker the French got, the better his position would be. Perhaps, if he negotiated now, in a few months he could send Leclerc packing, as he had Roume and before him Hédouville and Sonthonax.

The French general now wrote to Toussaint requesting that they meet in Le Cap. The black leader did not reply. Instead, one morning in May he got on his horse and rode toward the city with an escort of four hundred dragoons. The people of Le Cap, hearing Toussaint was coming, flocked into the streets. The blacks and many mulattoes cheered him, and some even knelt down as he passed by. Little girls threw flowers in his path. To the French it had all the appearance of a triumphant liberator entering the city he had liberated. They did not like it.

Not everyone cheered Toussaint. A few white planters standing in the crowd hissed as he rode by. Turning to his aide, the black leader said, "That is how men are. Those same whites who now insult me once crawled at my feet. They may still live to regret me."

Leclerc was having lunch aboard the flagship when he heard of Toussaint's arrival. He ordered the warships to fire a salute to the black leader, and hurried ashore to receive him.

The two men conferred in Leclerc's headquarters while Toussaint's dragoons surrounded the building and aides stood outside the conference room. "Well, General," Leclerc began, "we have the greatest admiration for the way you have borne the burden of governing Haiti. Our reconciliation will make this wonderful island blossom anew."

"Why did you bring sword and fire to Haiti?" Toussaint snapped, cutting off Leclerc. "This was a peaceful and prosperous island before you came!"

"Now, now," cooed Leclerc. "The sooner we forget the past, the sooner it will be mended. Each of us has done wrong. Let's rejoice in our reconciliation, General! Your staff and my officers will bear witness to our friendship."

Leclerc rose and left the room to invite all those assembled outside to enter. When he returned, he was holding the hand of Toussaint's youngest son, Saint-Jean. Although Toussaint had been assured his son was well, he had not seen him since he became a prisoner of the French.

Overjoyed, the black leader embraced his son and wept openly. As Leclerc had hoped, Toussaint's coldness vanished, and he accepted the French general's invitation to dine with him.

That evening Le Cap celebrated for the first time since the fire. Leclerc's personal residence, an old mansion that had not burned down, was filled with red roses, Toussaint's favorite flower. Important blacks, Frenchmen, Creoles and mulattoes all danced gracefully to the soft music of violins.

Toussaint sat in a place of honor, surrounded by French officers. During the dinner he refused the delicate wines and tempting dishes placed before him. Instead, he drank a glass of water and ate a bit of cheese, carefully cutting away all but the center of the piece. He had not come this far to be poisoned by the French.

After a few glasses of wine, General Leclerc, who was seated next to Toussaint, turned to the black leader and asked, "If the war had continued, General, where would you have got arms and supplies?"

"I would have taken them from you," Toussaint replied without hesitation.

Under the peace terms agreed on between Toussaint and Leclerc, France strongly affirmed that the blacks were to be free and equal, and the black army was to remain intact. But Toussaint was to hand over his power to the French and retire.

One morning soon after, the black leader summoned his troops before him. Standing stiffly in his blue and gold uniform, his voice heavy with sadness, he told his men it was time for him to retire. He praised them for their courage and loyalty, and said, "Never forget you are the guardians of your race and its honor."

Many of his men, among them the brave heroes of Crête-à-Pierrot, wept. Toussaint himself had difficulty controlling his emotion. After shaking hands with all his officers, he leaped onto his horse and headed toward Ennery.

The five thousand men Toussaint left behind watched more than the figure of a man on a horse disappear in the distance; they saw leave with Toussaint all the glory and honor of the fight for freedom. Eleven years ago they had risen up against their oppressors. Under Toussaint's leadership they had grown from an unruly band of half-naked ex-slaves into one of the most highly disciplined and capable armies in the world—an army that had routed the British and reduced the French army to shambles. And now . . . and now what? The future was a void. They did not know what the next hour would bring. Could the French be trusted? Would they give them equal rights as citizens as promised? Who would replace Toussaint as the champion of the people?

Only one thing did they feel sure of. Toussaint would never permit the French to restore slavery. If they tried, he would break out of retirement and strike them down.

Toussaint's youngest son and his stepson, Placide, accompanied him to Ennery, along with his staff. Suzanne and Isaac, who had been found hiding in the mountains, were already at the plantation. As the black leader neared Ennery, crowds of blacks and mulattoes came to meet him. They were not cheering now. They looked at him in reproachful silence, their eyes all asking the same question.

"Papa Toussaint! Papa Toussaint!" A woman bolder than the rest pushed through the crowd. "Have you forsaken us?"

The black leader stopped his horse. Looking down at his people and the woman who addressed him, he replied softly, "No, my child. Your brothers are still armed. All the officers have retained their posts. Toussaint will never forsake you."

Reunited again at Ennery, Toussaint's family put aside their sorrows and spent the evening enjoying their reunion. But Toussaint was not a man to let personal happiness distract him for long. The next morning he arose at dawn as usual and went to work with his staff. He had two main objectives in mind—to get his plantation back in order so it would once again be a model for all Haiti to emulate, and to keep a sharp eye on the French.

Every day Toussaint could be seen riding about his fields, talking to the laborers and checking on their work. Many black soldiers, unable to bear submission to the French, deserted the ranks. A number of them drifted toward Ennery, where they exchanged their arms for farm implements and went to work in the fields. Life at Ennery was tranquil and productive.

Shortly after the black leader had returned to Ennery, Dessalines arrived at the plantation. He was furious at Toussaint for submitting at a time when total victory seemed so near. He accused his former chief of cowardice, and said he would never lay down his arms to the French.

Unlike Toussaint, Dessalines preferred war to peace. He was in the war because he hated whites, and his goal had been and still was to rid Haiti of every last one of them. Now his former chief had ruined everything by submitting.

Toussaint did his best to calm the irate Dessalines, and urged him to surrender for the good of their people. Dessalines refused, seemingly unmoved by his former chief's pleas. Then, suddenly, he agreed.

The next day Dessalines set out for Le Cap at the head of five hundred dragoons. When he arrived in the city, the cry went up among the blacks, "Dessalines is here! Dessalines is here!"

The whites who heard the cry felt a tremor of aversion. Some felt fear, others just disgust, but none could resist a look at the dreaded "Tiger," Dessalines.

The whites put considerable pressure on Leclerc to arrest Dessalines. They would not rest until that "monster" was under lock and key. But Leclerc refused. Dessalines could perhaps serve a very useful purpose.

Unbeknown to the French general, Dessalines had some schemes of his own in which Leclerc would play a leading role. Both men, although they were not aware of it, now shared a common goal—the downfall of Toussaint Louverture.

Toussaint, concentrating on the French, neglected to keep

an eye on his generals. So, as the black leader went about his duties at Ennery, a new chapter in betrayal and perfidy began to unfold.

CHAPTER 16

AS Toussaint expected, the yellow fever toll rose higher and higher. By June, Leclerc was desperate. The rainy season still had several months to go, and already the hospitals were filled to overflowing. French soldiers were dropping dead on the streets.

Toussaint had contacts who kept a steady stream of information flowing in and out of Ennery. He knew the French forces were falling apart. And he knew time was on his side now. All he had to do was wait. Soon the French would be so weak they would be powerless against Toussaint, with most of his army and all the blacks of Haiti behind him. It would be a bloodless victory. Not a black would have been lost.

Another man, a very different man from Toussaint, was also assessing the situation. Dessalines, seeing the French weaken, thought, "Soon it will be time to strike—to get rid of the detested whites once and for all. Then I will declare independence."

Dessalines knew Toussaint would never agree to the violent plan he had in mind. His former chief was an obstacle. He decided Toussaint must be removed.

Since laying down his arms, Dessalines had been feigning devotion to Leclerc. He even rounded up black guerrillas who had refused to lay down their arms and slaughtered them with no more emotion than when he had murdered whites.

Leclerc was a little leery of his new ally. But France had no intention of keeping its agreement with Toussaint. Leclerc's orders were still the same: restore slavery. Until the black leader was out of the way, slavery could not be restored. And as long as the black army was strong, he could never get at Toussaint—unless, of course, someone like Dessalines would help.

Leclerc never doubted that he was the master and Dessalines the tool. When Dessalines came to him and urged his former chief's arrest, the French general was surprised, but delighted.

Early in June, Toussaint received a letter from a French general named Brunet, asking him to come to his headquarters on the Georges plantation. There were, Brunet wrote, important matters to settle, too complicated to discuss through correspondence.

Had he distrusted General Brunet, Toussaint would have been wily as a fox. But he knew the general to be an honest and trustworthy man, and the letter impressed him with its candid and respectful tone.

Besides, who would dare arrest Toussaint? The black army would rise up at once. The French were far too weak to risk catapulting Haiti into another war—a war that would surely be even more savage than the last.

A few days later, Toussaint and a small bodyguard arrived at General Brunet's home just as evening was falling. Embracing the black leader warmly, Brunet led him inside. Toussaint's bodyguard remained in the courtyard chatting with the French soldiers. The atmosphere was relaxed and casual.

"Your wife did not accompany you?" Brunet asked politely.

"No," replied Toussaint. "She sends you her regrets and hopes you will do us the honor of visiting our home someday soon."

"I would be delighted," said Brunet.

The two generals retired to the drawing room, and began discussing administrative problems. A soft knock at the door interrupted their conversation. Excusing himself, Brunet rose and opened the door.

Toussaint heard Brunet speak softly to whoever had knocked, but he could not make out what they said. Turning back to Toussaint, Brunet asked, "Will you excuse me a moment, General. An aide has just arrived with an urgent message."

"Of course," the black leader replied.

The door closed quietly, and Toussaint was left alone in the room. He had been somewhat ill the past few days, and now he was feeling unusually tired. The room began to grow dark. Toussaint rose from his chair and was lighting the candelabra when the door was suddenly kicked open. Ten French grenadiers, their bayonets drawn, rushed into the room.

Although startled, Toussaint acted without hesitation. He drew his sword and backed up against the wall, so that he faced all ten grenadiers.

"It's no use, General," shouted the officer in charge. "General Leclerc has ordered your arrest. Your men outside are in chains, and our soldiers are everywhere. If you resist, we will be forced to kill you. Your power in Haiti is at an end. Hand me your sword."

Enraged at such treachery, Toussaint demanded, "Where is General Brunet? I rely on the protection of General Brunet. He has given me his word of honor."

"General Brunet is not here," the officer replied.

"So he has hidden himself to escape my reproaches," said Toussaint scornfully.

The officer said nothing. Instead, he signaled his men to come forward and take Toussaint's sword. The soldiers then bound the black leader's hands behind his back, as they would a common outlaw, and hustled him into a carriage waiting outside. Surrounded by French soldiers, the carriage headed toward the harbor at Gonaïves.

None of the blacks who saw the carriage go by were suspicious. Had they known their leader was inside, bound like a criminal, they would have blocked the carriage's path with their bodies. But the French had been very careful. None of the blacks had any inkling of Toussaint's fate.

When the carriage reached Gonaïves, it was about midnight, and the streets were deserted. In a few minutes Toussaint was aboard the French warship *Créole*. There, to his dismay, he found his entire family under guard.

French soldiers had broken into Toussaint's home, stolen his money, jewels and papers and set fire to his fields. Members of his staff had been arrested, and any blacks who witnessed the deed were murdered. His family had then been herded into a carriage and aboard the *Créole*.

His voice shaking with anger, Toussaint demanded, "Why are they here? My family has no accounting whatever to give. I alone am responsible to the government. Their arrest is not justified!"

Several soldiers took hold of Toussaint, and began to lead him off to a cabin, where he would spend the entire voyage alone. As the soldiers took his arms, Toussaint turned and addressed a prophetic warning. "In overthrowing me, you have cut down only the trunk of the tree of liberty in Haiti. It will shoot up again, for its roots are many and deep."

While Haiti slept, innocent of this most treacherous and contemptible deed, the *Créole* lifted anchor and sailed noiselessly out of the harbor for France.

Haiti did not sleep for long. News of Toussaint's arrest and deportation spread through the colony. Overcome with grief, the blacks cried out in rage against the French, whom they now despised more than ever.

In the mountains, so long silent, the drums were heard again, summoning the blacks to rise up and avenge this most monstrous crime against their race.

The guerrillas who had deserted the regular troops rather than lay down their arms to the French were the first to respond. Sweeping down from the hills, they hurled themselves on the French at Ennery, Plaisance and Dondon. Everywhere insurrections broke out. General Belair, a nephew of Toussaint's, came forth to take his uncle's place and lead the blacks against the insidious French.

Leclerc was prepared. This was the reaction he anticipated and the reason why he could never have risked such a move without two formidable weapons on his side—Dessalines and Christophe.

Dessalines was still pretending allegiance to Leclerc and waiting for the yellow fever to further decimate the French forces. When the time came to strike, he knew he could count on Christophe.

Leclerc ordered the two black generals to suppress the uprising and round up the leaders. With ruthless efficiency, they carried out their orders. General Belair was captured and, side by side with his courageous wife, faced the French firing squad.

Suppressed by their own generals and lacking leaders, the blacks became confused, and the uprising foundered. It had all gone according to plan. Toussaint was out of the way, and Christophe and Dessalines had the rebels under control. Leclerc breathed easier. Now, with utmost care, he had to plan the next difficult step—the restoration of slavery.

He ordered Christophe and Dessalines to disarm the laborers, and soldiers spread out over the colony, confiscating weapons. The blacks were angry and frightened. Had not Toussaint told them their muskets were their liberty?

Then, in July, news arrived which set Haiti afire. France had restored slavery in the nearby colony of Guadeloupe!

All doubt about French intentions in Haiti was swept away. Toussaint's arrest, the disarming of the laborers and now the news from Guadeloupe added up to only one ugly word in the blacks' minds—*slavery!*

Nothing could keep the blacks down now. The uprising was so widespread that Dessalines and Christophe decided it was time to change sides again, and the rebels needed their help too much to refuse it. Old sins were forgiven as all the blacks joined together in a united front against the common enemy.

Leclerc, enormously distressed at this turn of events, wrote Napoleon, "The blacks have learned of your plans for the colonies. If you wish to preserve Haiti, send a new army and, above all, money. If you do not, Haiti is lost. Once it is lost, you will never regain it."

In almost no time, the two generals who had betrayed Toussaint were the leaders of the new uprising—and their rallying cry was, ironically, the name of Toussaint Louverture!

And where was the man whose name was their rallying cry and a symbol of freedom to blacks all over the world?

Throughout the entire voyage to France, Toussaint had been kept in carefully guarded isolation. When the ship dropped anchor at Brest, he was allowed to bid his family good-bye. Then, as he stood by helplessly, Suzanne and his sons were led away to an unknown place of confinement in France. The black leader himself was imprisoned in the citadel of Brest.

Toussaint lost no time in protesting his treatment. "I demand a trial!" he wrote Napoleon.

But Leclerc warned Napoleon, "Toussaint's trial and execution would only further inflame the blacks. He must be put in prison where he can never escape and return to Haiti. His influence here is that of a religious chief."

Napoleon accepted Leclerc's advice.

Near the border between France and Switzerland were the stark and rugged Jura Mountains. Here, eight months of the year, the sheer, rocky cliffs were covered with snow and ice. Heavy gray clouds hung over the solitary peaks, obscuring the sun for days on end. In the winter, when temperatures dropped way below zero, freezing winds whipped and wailed around the thick stone walls of an old feudal castle—Fort de Joux, now a prison reserved for Napoleon's most dangerous adversaries.

It was to this grim, bitterly cold prison that Napoleon sent Toussaint, a man who had spent all his life on a sun-washed tropical island.

When Toussaint arrived at Fort de Joux, it was late August. Already there was a sharp chill in the air. Shivering in his lightweight general's uniform, the black leader was led through the thick, heavy door of the castle, down long, gloomy corridors, into a tomblike room that was to be his cell.

The guards withdrew, and the iron door to his cell clanged shut. Toussaint looked around at the room that was to be his home for the indefinite future. The stone floor was cold and damp, with little puddles of water here and there; the thick walls oozed and dripped; everything in the room was clammy. Through the tiny barred window, he could barely see a piece of the gray sky. A crude little fireplace was the only source of heat.

No one was permitted to see Toussaint but the commandant of the fort, a man named Baille. He was allowed no communication from the outside, and Baille was forbidden to give him any news of Haiti.

The commandant was a reasonably humane man, and very proud to have such a famous prisoner in his charge. At first he even indulged Toussaint somewhat—giving him sugar from his own pantry and lending the black leader his personal secretary so he could dictate his memoirs.

But Toussaint was now about fifty-eight, and almost from the first week in the clammy prison, his health began to suffer. A man of action, accustomed to a sunny climate and vigorous physical activity, he found confinement to a small, chilly cell almost unendurable.

As the weeks went by and the weather grew colder, Toussaint kept a fire going all the time. Still, he could never get warm. Every morning, when Baille appeared with a day's supply of salt meat, cheese and bread, he found Toussaint huddled over the fire, shivering.

The black leader became increasingly gloomy. He was worried about his family, his people and his own failing health. Not knowing what was occurring in Haiti was torture to him. Certainly the French intended to restore slavery. Why else would they have arrested him? He was equally certain his people would resist. "They'll give up their lives before they'll give up their liberty," he warned Napoleon.

Toussaint knew his people. At that moment Leclerc was writing the First Consul, "There is a veritable fanaticism in this most recent insurrection. The blacks fight with a fervor that is unbelievable. They laugh at death, even the women. They allow themselves to be killed down to the last man, but they never surrender."

Napoleon sent thousands of additional soldiers, but Leclerc kept begging for more. In September he reported, "My entire army is destroyed, even the reinforcements you sent. Every day the forces of the rebels grow stronger, while mine grow weaker."

Toussaint had warned the French that in arresting him they were cutting down only the trunk of the tree, not the roots. Now, all over Haiti, new leaders sprang up to take his place. "It was not enough to remove Toussaint," Leclerc realized too late. "There are *two thousand* leaders to be removed!"

The ravages of yellow fever and the fanatic resistance of the blacks were making Toussaint's prediction come true—Haiti was rapidly turning into the image of hell the French so richly deserved.

Leclerc became frantic. The intolerable climate, the deadly fever, his army disappearing before his eyes—it was too much for any man. His health began to decline and he was given to fits of despair and melancholy. He begged to be relieved of his post, and finally he too fell victim to the dreaded yellow fever. He was only thirty years old. The last words he uttered before he died were a curse against the ill-fated expedition which had brought him to this bloody land.

While her husband fought the rebels, Pauline had kept up a steady stream of balls and parties, flitting from one love affair to another. Now, left alone in the nightmare that was Haiti, she was stricken with grief and remorse. She cut off her long flaxen hair and placed it in her husband's coffin. Then Pauline and the body of Leclerc left for France, leaving behind the colony they had come to conquer—Leclerc by his sword, Pauline by her charms.

Two months later, Napoleon stood over the coffin containing the body of Leclerc, his brother-in-law. As Pauline wept softly, the First Consul said, "Here is all that remains of that fine army—the body of a general, my right arm, now a handful of dust. All has perished. Fatal conquest! Cursed land!"

The cruel and sadistic General Rochambeau succeeded

Leclerc. Napoleon sent twenty thousand more soldiers, and Rochambeau began to wage a war of total extermination against the blacks. Military honor, the ethics of war, humane treatment of prisoners, all the values Toussaint lived by, were unknown to a man like Rochambeau. When he couldn't defeat the blacks in battle, he resorted to sadistic practices that rivaled any of the tortures the former slaveowners had thought up.

But even these excesses could not destroy the resistance of the blacks. They returned blow for blow.

Dessalines was in his element now. Toussaint's subtle methods of warfare—his use of military pressure to force the French to negotiate—had confused him. The savagery of the French was something else. That he could deal with. Rochambeau murdered five hundred blacks? Dessalines would murder five hundred whites and hang their bodies from trees along the road to Le Cap.

Toussaint, languishing in his prison cell, was spared the news from Haiti. The slaughter and excesses on both sides would have reduced him to total despair. And the desperate, almost superhuman heroism of his people would have broken his heart. He had worked so hard to save them from this bloody nightmare, and now it was a reality.

In the Jura Mountains, in the year 1803, spring came late, as usual. Toussaint had been in prison over seven months. The long winter had played havoc with his health. He developed a fever and severe cough that racked his whole body and kept him confined to bed much of the time. One day blood appeared on his handkerchief.

The commandant Baille had been replaced by a heartless man named Amiot. Like Baille, he had been ordered to let no one see Toussaint. He carried out his orders with such excessive zeal he refused to allow even a physician into Toussaint's cell.

On the morning of April 7, Toussaint felt well enough to get out of bed. Although extremely weak, he managed to make a fire and brew a few herbs. On Napoleon's orders, Amiot had cut down his wood supply, and often he had no fire at all.

As he sat in his cold cell drinking the brew, Toussaint's thoughts strayed, as usual, to Haiti. In his mind's eye he could see the sun-bleached beaches and the tropical skies. Although shivering uncontrollably, he could remember what the hot sun felt like, and the soft trade winds blowing in from the sea. He recalled the glorious times riding through the countryside and seeing the once-scorched earth coming to life again—coffee trees ripening, lemon trees in bloom, sugarcane blowing in the breeze. He could close his eyes and see his people working in the fields—free people, people without fear who turned and waved at him as he rode by. Those had been good days, and his people had risen to such glorious heights . . . before the French came.

A few hours later Amiot entered the cell. He found Toussaint slumped in his chair, the brew spilled on the floor beside him.

Napoleon had what he wanted—Toussaint's life. But the black leader was more than a man—he was a nation. And Napoleon knew that. In taking Toussaint's life, he had hoped to destroy the soul of black Haiti. Napoleon was to learn the hard way that neither the soul of black Haiti nor the soul of black freedom was destructible.

EPILOGUE

Toussaint's death, far from destroying the blacks' morale, spurred them on to even more incredible feats of heroism. In their desperate fight to preserve liberty, they exhibited a heroism and self-sacrifice unexcelled in recorded history. Every

Toussaint of Haiti

able-bodied black man, woman and child threw himself into the fight with no thought of personal danger. Each time a leader was killed, a new one came forth to take his place.

One of Rochambeau's generals commented, "This is no war. It is a fight of tigers! One has to be transported by frenzy to keep it up."

When the tide finally turned against Rochambeau's army, it was not the ferocity of Dessalines that was responsible. It was the people—the courageous blacks and mulattoes who hated violence as much as Dessalines and Rochambeau loved it. And it was the black army—the army Toussaint had trained to hold its own against the finest soldiers in Europe.

One of Rochambeau's generals wrote home, "What men these blacks are! How they fight and die! I have seen a solid column, torn apart by the shot of four cannons, advance without taking one step backward. And they advanced singing! Can you imagine the effect of that song—two thousand voices raised in unison with the sound of cannon as the bass? One must see such bravery to believe it possible."

In the face of such bravery, Rochambeau's army crumbled just as Leclerc's had. In November of 1803, seven months after Toussaint's death, Rochambeau and the French admitted defeat.

The long rebellion which had started on a sultry night in August of 1791, and which had woven its way through wars with the British, the Spanish and the French, was over. It was the only successful slave revolt in history.

Christophe, Dessalines and the other leaders drew up a declaration of independence, and the Republic of Haiti—the first independent black nation in history—was born.

The white was removed from the French tricolor flag, and above the city of Le Cap was raised the red and blue flag of free Haiti, inscribed with the words "Liberty or Death."

Napoleon's dream of a French colonial empire in the New

World was finished. The expedition had been one of the worst disasters of his career. It had cost the lives of over sixty thousand French soldiers and probably twice that many blacks. Without Haiti as a base of operations, the Louisiana Territory was useless to him.

The United States had followed events in Haiti very carefully. President Jefferson knew that if Napoleon's troops conquered Haiti and moved on to Louisiana, the United States would be forced into an alliance with England against France. A major war would almost certainly have followed.

The stubborn resistance of Haiti's blacks changed the entire trend of events. By spring of 1803, Napoleon's treasury had been drained by the war in Haiti. He was once again on the brink of war with England, and he needed money. Fearing that Haiti was lost, he decided to sell Louisiana to the United States for fifteen million dollars, and turn his search for new conquests elsewhere. In May he plunged France back into war with England.

Thanks to Toussaint Louverture and the invincible blacks of Haiti, the United States was no longer threatened by war with France. With the Louisiana Purchase, for which Toussaint and his people were at least indirectly responsible, the United States more than doubled its territory. The new democracy, which now stretched from Canada to the Gulf of Mexico, was no longer threatened by Napoleon's schemes for a New World Empire. The First Consul had turned his greedy eyes elsewhere.

Years later, when Napoleon was in exile on Saint Helena, he wrote in his memoirs, "I regret my attitude toward Haiti. It was a bad mistake to try and force it into submission. I should have contented myself with letting Toussaint Louverture govern it."

Had Napoleon allowed Toussaint to rule, Haiti would

almost certainly have become the enlightened progressive nation the black leader dreamed of—a nation where different races lived side by side, prosperous, free and equal.

But the men who succeeded Toussaint took Haiti down the very path he so dreaded. In 1804 Dessalines had himself crowned emperor of Haiti, and the following year he ordered all the whites massacred. For generations whites were banished from Haiti. The Creoles whom Toussaint befriended, and who in turn rejoiced in his downfall, did indeed live to regret him, as the black leader had predicted.

Dessalines ruled so despotically the blacks finally murdered him. Christophe then became king of Haiti, and attempted to establish an enlightened rule. But he was not the man for the task, and when revolts broke out he committed suicide.

Weakened and torn apart by so many years of war and destruction, Haiti fell easy prey to one despot after another and to exploitation by various colonial powers.

Today Haiti is one of the most tyrannical and bloodthirsty dictatorships in the world. Its people wallow in poverty and disease, while military police prowl the countryside and an aging despot rides about in a bullet-proof car, a rifle in his hand. Anyone who voices a protest today may disappear tomorrow.

This is not the Haiti that Toussaint loved and died for. It is not the Haiti thousands of blacks gladly surrendered their lives for. They died for liberty, so they and their children would never again be oppressed and tyrannized.

But as the soul of black freedom is not destructible, so the Haiti they fought for is not dead. Perhaps all that is needed is a leader—a great man who will "raise the sacred standard of liberty and gather around him his companions in misfortune." Perhaps all that is needed is another Toussaint Louverture.

SUGGESTED FURTHER READING

Beard, Rev. John R. *Toussaint L'Ouverture: a Biography and Autobiography.* Boston, James Redpath, 1863.

Davis, Harold P. *Black Democracy.* Dodge Publishing Co., 1936; reprint, Canada, Biblo & Tanner, 1966.

Hazard, Samuel. *Santo Domingo, Past and Present, with a Glance at Hayti.* New York, Harper & Bros., 1873.

James, C. L. R. *The Black Jacobins: Toussaint L'Ouverture and the San Domingo Revolution.* New York, Vintage Books, 1963 (paperback).

Korngold, Ralph. *Citizen Toussaint.* New York, Hill and Wang, 1965 (paperback).

Leyburn, James T. *The Haitian People.* New Haven, Yale University Press, 1966.

Moran, Charles. *Black Triumvirate.* New York, Exposition Press, 1957.

Mossell, Charles W. *Toussaint L'Ouverture: the Hero of Santo Domingo, Soldier, Statesman, Martyr.* Lockport, New York, Ward & Cobb, 1896.

Waxman, Percy. *The Black Napoleon.* New York, Harcourt, Brace & Co., 1931.

INDEX

Africa, 13; Toussaint's dream of freeing, 125. *See also* Guerrilla-warfare tactics; Slaves; Voodoo
Agé (General), 111, 112, 149
Agriculture, crops, 11, 121; Toussaint works to restore, 61–62, 116–18
America. *See* United States
American Revolution, 21, 22, 64
Amiot (French commandant), 179–80
Arada tribe, 13
Arawaks, 9–10
Armies. *See* Arms; British; French Expeditionary Army; Rebel army; Spanish
Arms, 29, 34, 36, 37, 40, 44, 58–59, 62, 70–71, 78, 79, 83, 92, 99, 100, 117, 118, 130, 167
Artibonite Valley, 72
Austria, 43

Baille (French commandant), 176–77, 179
Baptiste, Pierre, 13–14, 15, 19, 33, 120
Beauvais (mulatto general), 72
Belair, Charles, 98, 174
Bel-Argent (horse), 128
Biassou, 34, 35, 37, 38, 39, 40, 42, 44, 52, 53, 57–58, 60–61
Big Whites, 19–20
Black Code, 22
Blacks, freedman appointed to government post, 48; of United States, 115; casualties of rebellion, 116, 182; living conditions after rebellion, 116–20. *See also* Laborers; Maroons; Slaves; Specific entries
Bois Caïman (glade), 27–28

Bonaparte. *See* Josephine; Leclerc, Pauline; Napoleon I
Borgella, Bernard, 123–26
Boukman (rebel leader), 27, 28, 29, 31–32, 34
Brandicourt (French colonel), 46
Bréda, Count de, 13, 14–15
Bréda (plantation), 11, 12, 13, 20, 26, 29, 30, 31, 32, 33, 49
Brest, France, 175
British, 135, 182; declare war on France, 43; alliance with Spain, 54–55; and restoration of slavery, 54, 62, 67; invade Haiti, 54; conquest of Haiti by imminent, 55; Toussaint's victories against, 58; army reinforced after Spain surrenders, 61; stir up insurrections, 62; mulattoes' hatred of, 64; Toussaint's assault against, 70–73; surrender to Toussaint, 77; trade treaty with Toussaint, 78–79, 90–91, 96; cost of ill-fated expedition, 79; negotiations with Toussaint, 88; make peace with France, 134; new war with France, 182
Brunet (French general), 171–73
Buccaneers, 10
Bush tactics. *See* Guerrilla-warfare tactics

Caesar, Julius, 20
Cahos Mountains, 156
Ça Ira, 159
Canada, 135, 182
Cap François. *See* Le Cap
Caribbean, 43, 55, 76, 99, 135
Catholicism, 14, 15, 28, 119
Christophe, Henri, 67, 130–31, 140, 142–45, 147, 148, 149–50, 154, 156, 164–65, 174–75, 181, 183
"Circles," 122, 123

185

Civil war, 67, 97; American, 115. *See also* War of the Knives
Coisnon (Abbé), 152, 153
Colonial Assembly, 23, 38, 39, 41, 42, 48
Colonists. *See* Colonial Assembly; Creoles; Mulattoes; Whites
Columbus Christopher, 9, 111
Constitution (of Haiti), 124–28, 129, 131, 134
Consulate (French), 106
Counterrevolutionaries, 48. *See also* Royalists
Courts, 118
Créole (warship), 173–74
Creole language, 14
Creoles, described, 6, 11, 17, 18–19; first in Haiti, 10; join royalists, 49–50; flee Haiti, 50, 51–52; welcome British, 54; massacred, 181. *See also* Colonial Assembly; Planters; Whites
Crête-à-Pierrot, 156–60, 167
Crops. *See* Agriculture; Trade
Cultivators. *See* Laborers
Culture. *See* Education; Theater

Damballa (voodoo god), 27–28
Democracy, birth of, 43
Dessalines, Jean Jacques, 67, 92, 98, 100, 103, 104–06, 130, 132, 150, 156–58, 159, 169, 170–71, 174–75, 179, 181, 183
Directory (French), 78, 85, 86, 89, 106
Dominican Republic, 11. *See also* Santo Domingo
Dominion status, 124, 127
Dondon, 111, 112, 174

Economy, restored by Toussaint, 116–19. *See also* Agriculture; Trade
Education, of Toussaint, 14, 15, 20–21; of Creoles, 18; of mulattoes, 23; of blacks under Toussaint, 119, 120
Elba, 135

Emancipation. *See* Slavery, abolition of
England. *See* British
Ennery, 89, 90, 120, 151, 153, 167, 168, 169, 170, 174
Epictetus, 20
Equal rights, for mulattoes, 25, 48, 122; for whites, 122; for all citizens, 126; for blacks, 167, 168. *See also* Slavery, abolition of
Espinville, Marquis d', 59–60
Europeans, 9. *See also* specific nationalities
Exports. *See* Trade

Fort Dauphin, 149
Fort de Joux, 176
Fort Picolet, 145
French, settle Haiti, 10–11; Haiti ceded to, 10–11; government in Haiti, 22; attempt to suppress slave rebellion, 42–43; stop assault on rebels, 43; offer amnesty, 44; Toussaint fights against, 44–47; British advances against, 54; army in Haiti collapsing, 54–55; abolish slavery, 56; Toussaint joins, 56–57; peace treaty with Spain, 60; Santo Domingo ceded to, 60; political trends in France, 78; relations with Toussaint deteriorate, 78–81; retain control of Haiti over British, 79; schemes to get rid of Toussaint, 85, 89–91; disband rebel army, 91–92; special agent ousted, 92–93; instigate civil war, 93–94; Napoleon in power, 106; make peace in Europe, 129–30, 134; peace terms with Toussaint, 167; defeated in Haiti, 181; sell Louisiana Territory, 182. *See also* Directory; Napoleon I; National Assembly; National Convention; Slavery, restoration of
French Expeditionary Army, planned, 134; warnings against sending, 135, 137; Napoleon's reasons for sending, 135–36; de-

Index

scribed, 136–37, 140, 141; reaches Santo Domingo, 140; Napoleon's phases for, 141, 150; advances of, 142–49, 153; role of Toussaint's sons, 150–53; repelled at Snake Gully, 154–56; attacks Crête-à-Pierrot, 156–59; harassment by Toussaint, 160–61; suffers losses, 162–63, 170; Christophe surrenders to, 164–65; Toussaint comes to terms with, 165–67; decimated by yellow fever, 170; Toussaint captured by, 172–73; uprising against, 174–75, 177–79, 180–81; reinforced, 177, 179; defeated, 181; cost of, 182
French Revolution, 21–22, 25, 26, 42, 44, 48, 49, 55, 56, 78, 136, 141
French Revolutionary Wars, 43, 44, 79, 134, 136; Toussaint's role in, 79
Friends of the Blacks, 25

Galbaud (governor), 48–50, 51
Gaou-Ginou, 12, 13
García, Don Joachim, 47, 53, 111, 112, 113–14
George III (King of England), 77, 129
Georges Plantation, 171
Gonaïves, 109, 110, 153, 154, 173
Government (of Haiti), under France, 22; Toussaint reorganizes, 118; staffed by blacks and whites, 119. *See also* Colonial Assembly
Grande Anse, 72
Great Britain. *See* British
Guadeloupe, 175
Guerrilla-warfare tactics, 13, 37, 40, 47, 58, 157–58, 159, 160–61

Haiti (colony), society of, 6, 23–24; Columbus discovers, 9; climate, 9; described, 9, 128–29, 180; settled by Europeans, 9–11; ceded to France, 10–11; population, 19, 23, 116; provinces, 20; government, 22. *See also* specific entries

Haiti, Republic of, 181, 183
Hédouville, Count d', 85–89, 91, 92–95, 96, 100, 104
Hermonas, Marquis d', 47
Herrara (Spanish general), 112–13
Hispaniola, 9, 10, 113
Holland, 43
Hôtel de la République, 119

Independence, Toussaint's attitude toward, 80, 115, 127, 138–39; declared, 181. *See also* Self-rule
Insurrection. *See* Slave rebellion
Integrated society, Toussaint's desire for, 122
Ireland, 113

Jacmel, 99–101
Jamaica, 76, 90–91
Jean-François, 34, 35, 36, 37–38, 39, 40, 42, 44, 52, 53, 57–58, 60–61
Jeannot, 34–36
Jefferson, Thomas, 136, 182
Jérémie, 54, 72, 76
Josephine Bonaparte, 135
Jura Mountains, 176, 179

Laborers, 62, 74; march on Le Cap, 67, 92, 109–10; pay of, 116, 117–18; forced to remain on one plantation, 117; response to Toussaint's policies, 118; response to Moyse's execution, 133–34; armed, 137; join rebel army, 160; disarmed, 175
Lacroix, Pamphile de, 148, 159, 162
Lamartinière (mulatto general), 158, 159
Language, 14
Laveaux, Comte de, 44, 48, 49, 50, 51, 54, 56, 58, 61, 64–70, 79, 80–81, 82, 96
Law, 22, 118
Lebrun (French aide), 142–44
Le Cap, 5, 6, 30, 51, 54, 84, 98, 109, 164, 179, 181; described, 17, 143; Galbaud and royalists take, 49–

187

50; burning of, 50, 145–47, 149, 151; mulattoes take, 65–68, 69; laborers march on, 67, 92, 109–10; Toussaint's triumphant entry into, 68; Hédouville forced out of, 92–93; Roume ousted from, 111; reconstructed under Toussaint, 118–19; scene of constitution's proclamation, 125–26; taken by French, 142–47; evacuated, 144–47; Toussaint enters to surrender, 165–66; Dessalines enters to surrender, 169

Leclerc, Charles Victor Emmanuel, 141, 152, 161; heads French expedition, 136, 140; warned about Toussaint, 137; takes Le Cap, 142–47; moves to capture Toussaint, 150–51, 153, 156; at Crête-à-Pierrot, 156, 159, 160; loses many men, 162, 170; wants to end war, 163; bribes Christophe to surrender, 164; requests Toussaint to surrender, 165; makes peace with Toussaint, 166–67; alliance with Dessalines, 169, 170–71; becomes desperate, 170; suppresses uprising, 174; disarms blacks, 174; new uprising against, 174–75, 177–78; advises prison for Toussaint, 176; death, 178

Leclerc, Pauline, 141, 142, 178
Les Cayes, 100, 103
Libertas, Bayon de, 15, 17, 20, 30, 33
Libertas, Madame de, 30, 32–33
Limbé, 67
L'Indien (frigate), 84
Little Whites, 19–20, 41
Louis XVI (King of France), 22, 43, 45
Louisiana Territory, 135–36, 182
Louverture, François Dominique Toussaint: chronology of life, birth, 12; adopts name Louverture, 12; childhood, 12, 14; education, 14, 15, 20–21; baptized, 15; teens, 15; put in charge of stable, 15; made coachman, 17; marriage, 19; made steward of livestock, 20; sons, 20; takes charge of Bréda, 30; leaves Bréda, 32–34; joins slave rebellion, 34; made physician to rebel army, 35; role in rebels' peace offer, 37–38; takes title of brigadier-general, 39; begins training rebels, 40; heads own army, 40–41; retreats from French, 42–43; joins Spanish, 44–45; defeats French under Brandicourt, 46–47; proposes Spanish free slaves, 47; makes plea for black unity, 52; victories against French, 52–53; begins freeing slaves, 53; grows uneasy over alliance with Spanish, 53–54, 55; joins French, 56–57; appointed commander of the Cordon of the West, 56–57; routs Biassou and Jean-François, 57–58; victories against British and Spanish, 58; defeats Spanish under Marquis d'Espinville, 59–60; becomes undisputed leader of blacks, 61; works to restore agriculture, 61–62; wins trust of blacks and whites, 62–64, 68; friendship with Laveaux, 64–65; rescues Laveaux and puts down mulatto coup, 66–68; appointed lieutenant governor of Haiti, 69; launches assault against British, 70–73; triumphant entry into Port-au-Prince, 73–75; warns Jamaica against interference, 76; defeats British, 76–77, 79; accepts trade treaty with British, 78–79; fears France, 78–79; moves toward self-rule, 80; requests Laveaux's departure, 80–81; appointed commander-in-chief, 82; ousts Sonthonax, 82–85; relationship with Hédouville, 86–89; submits "resignation," 89; rejects French request to invade United States and Jamaica, 90–91; signs trade treaties with

Index

United States and British, 91; forces out Hédouville, 92–93; problems with Rigaud and mulattoes 94–97; fights War of the Knives, 98–102; defeats Rigaud and mulattoes, 103; orders mulatto troops purged, 104; reputation as humane conqueror damaged, 106; warns Napoleon against restoring slavery, 107–08; annexation of Santo Domingo, 108–13; ousts Roume, 111–12; controls all Hispaniola, 113; frees slaves and revives economy of Santo Domingo, 114; begins building black republic, 114–15; restores agriculture, 116–18; rebuilds Haiti, 118–19; inspection tours of Haiti, 120–22; and race problem, 122; entertains at government palace, 122, 123; draws up constitution, 124–28; becomes governor and dictator of Haiti, 128–9; criticized by Napoleon, 129; prepares for French invasion, 130, 137; neglects people's discontent, 130; his officers' antagonism, 130–31; puts down Moyse's revolt, 132; executes Moyse, 133; represses dissent, 134; deports some whites, 138; pleads with Napoleon for Haiti, 139; views arrival of French expedition, 140; goes to Le Cap, 141, 146–47; plans strategy to repel French, 147–50; his generals oppose his strategy, 148; meets with his sons, 151–53; receives letter from Napoleon, 151–52; repels French at "Snake Gully," 154–56; garrison at Crête-à-Pierrot, 156; harasses French, 160–61; his position grows stronger, 162; decides to negotiate, 163–64; makes peace with Leclerc, 165–67; retires, 167–70; accepts Brunet's invitation, 171; captured by French and deported, 172–74; imprisonment, 175–77, 179–80; warns French, 178; death, 180; Napoleon regrets attitude toward, 182; successors to, 183; **Personal description**, attitude toward violence, 15, 28, 31, 35–36, 39, 60, 63, 73, 76, 82–83, 105–06, 111, 163; personality and character, 16–17, 45–46, 65, 86, 98, 102, 128, 133; physical appearance, 17, 68; military ability and tactics, 20, 40–41, 42, 44–46, 53, 58–60, 61, 67, 70–73, 76, 98–100, 109, 113, 115, 130, 137, 147–50, 154–56, 160–62, 179; political and diplomatic abilities, 20, 44, 52, 76–79, 85, 86, 88–91, 92, 101, 109–10, 115, 122, 163, 164–65, 179; dress of, 35, 53, 75, 113, 126; as humane conqueror, 45–46, 60, 61, 63, 71–72, 73, 99, 100, 101, 103–04, 106, 114, 133; attitude toward whites, 62, 63, 64, 83, 119, 122, 137–38; as peacemaker, 68, 81–82, 92, 94, 95, 96, 97, 101, 122; administrative abilities of, 114–23; as just ruler, 118, 122, 127, 133–34; on his plantation, 120; physical strength of, 121–23, 147, 177, 179–80; eating and sleeping habits of, 121–22

Louverture, Genevieve, 15
Louverture, Isaac, 20, 120, 150–53, 168, 173, 175
Louverture, Paul, 33, 57, 58, 67, 114, 140, 150
Louverture, Placide, 20, 120, 150–53, 168, 173, 175
Louverture, Saint-Jean, 20, 120, 153, 166, 168, 173, 175
Louverture, Suzanne, 19–20, 32, 33–34, 89, 90, 120, 151, 153, 168, 173, 175

Macandal, 5–7, 15, 25, 27
Magi, 16
Maitland (British general), 71, 73, 76–78, 88, 89
Maréchaussée, 5–6
Marmelade, 161–62

189

Maroons, 6, 7, 27, 34, 98, 99
Marseillaise, 159
Mexico, Gulf of, 182
Michel, Pierre, 66, 67
Military. *See* Arms; French Expeditionary Army; Guerrilla-warfare tactics; Louverture, Toussaint; Rebel army
Mirebelais, 59-60
Mississippi River, 136
Môle St.-Nicholas, 72, 76, 77, 98
Molière (Catholic priest), 125
Money unit, 118
Morne Pélé, 42
Morne-Rouge, 27
Moyse (General), 67, 71, 84-85, 91-92, 93, 95, 109, 111, 130-34, 148
Mulattoes, described, 6, 23; discrimination against, 23, 24, 48; number of, 23; Ogé's insurrection, 24-25, 26; relation with blacks, 25, 30, 42, 94-106, 121; France grants equality to, 25, 48; revolt in West and South, 41-42; attitude toward French and British, 64; army of, 64, 98, 104-06; attitude toward Toussaint, 64, 69, 128; Toussaint's attitude toward, 69, 94, 97; Rigaud stirs trouble among, 94-97; War of the Knives, 98-103, 107; Toussaint purges, 104; Dessalines massacres, 104-06; Toussaint works toward harmony with, 122; response to French expedition, 143, 149; fight French, 154, 158-59, 181. *See also* Rigaud

Napoleon I, 106, 112, 115, 163; plans to restore slavery, 107, 130, 134-35; placates Toussaint, 108; angered by Toussaint, 112; and Toussaint's constitution, 124-25, 127-28, 129; schemes for Haiti and New World, 135-36, 175; deceives his soldiers, 136, 141, 159; ignores Toussaint's pleas for Haiti, 139; attempts to deceive blacks, 141; deceives United States, 142; uses Toussaint's sons as decoys, 150-51; writes Toussaint, 151-52; angered by Leclerc's failure, 162; imprisons Toussaint, 176; sends reinforcements, 177, 179; curses Haiti, 178; role in Toussaint's death, 180; dreams for Haiti and New World ended, 182. *See also* French Expeditionary Army
National Assembly (French), 23, 24
National Convention (French), 55-56, 78
Negroes. *See* Blacks
Netherlands, 43
New World, 9, 10, 90; Napoleon's schemes for, 135-36, 142, 181-82. *See also* specific entries
Northern Plain, 29, 31-32

Ogé, Vincent, 24-25, 26, 41

Paris, France, 21, 25, 64, 150, 151
Paris, Peace of, 135
"Paris of the Antilles." *See* Le Cap
Pauline (Toussaint's mother), 13, 14
Pélagie (Toussaint's stepmother), 14, 120
Pétion (mulatto general), 100
Petit-Goâve, 98
Pinchinat (mulatto leader), 41
Pirates, 10, 114
Place de Royale, 6
Plantations, owners of, 11; houses described, 18; burned in rebellion, 32; government takes over, 116, 117. *See also* Agriculture; Bréda
Planters, Toussaint's treatment of, 62, 63, 64, 116, 117; response to Toussaint's policies, 118. *See also* Creoles
Place d'Armes, 68, 125-26
Plaisance, 174
Port-au-Prince, 41, 60, 72, 97, 98, 123, 149; Toussaint's triumphant entry into, 73-75
Port-de-Paix, 54, 150

Index

Rainy season, 71, 73, 149, 162, 165, 170
Ravine-à-Couleuvres, 154–56, 160
Raynal, Abbé, 20–21, 68
Rebel army, described, 34, 42, 45, 59, 68, 74, 167–68; leaders of, 34–35, 39, 61; early tactics, 36–37; makes peace offer, 37–38; military training, 39–41; size of, 40, 42, 58, 68, 70, 147; fighting ability of, 58–59, 76, 113, 181; morale of, 59, 160; whites' treatment by, 63; France's schemes to get rid of, 89–92; casualty figures, 116, 182; Christophe and Dessalines head, 175. *See also* Arms; Guerrilla-warfare tactics; Slave rebellion
Rebellion. *See* Slave rebellion; French Expeditionary Army
Religion. *See* Catholicism; Voodoo
Rigaud, André, 64, 65–66, 69, 70, 72, 94–104, 107
Rochambeau, vicomte de, 149, 154–56, 159, 178–79, 181
Roume (French commissioner), 96, 97, 108–10, 111–12
Royalists, 25, 45, 48, 62, 64. *See also* British; Spanish
Ryswick, Treaty of, 10

St. Domingo, 10
Saint Domingue, 10
Saint Helena, 182
St.-Marc, 150
Samana Bay, 139
San Domingo, 10
Santo Domingo (city), 111
Santo Domingo (colony), 139; early history, 10–11; Toussaint joins, 44–47; ceded to France, 60; Toussaint annexes, 108–14; economy revived by Toussaint, 114; French expedition reaches, 140; surrenders to French, 150
Self-rule, 80, 124, 126
Slave rebellion, planned, 27–28; begins, 29–31; falters, 32, 35, 37–38; Toussaint joins, 34; cordoned off by whites, 41; spreads, 41–42; French attempt to suppress, 42–43; French drop assault, 43; suppression of ended, 43; loss of life and property from, 116; new uprising, 174–75, 177–79, 180–81; succeeds, 81. *See also* French Expeditionary Army; Rebel army
Slavery, in Santo Domingo, 34, 108, 109; in Jamaica, 76, 90, 91; in United States, 90, 91, 115; world's attitude toward, 115
Slavery, abolition of, Toussaint proposes to Spanish, 47; Sonthonax declares, 51, 52; responses to, 51, 52, 53, 54; France affirms, 56; by Toussaint in Santo Domingo, 110
Slavery, restoration of, by British, 54, 62, 67; by French, 78, 107–08, 130, 134–35, 141, 171, 175, 177. *See also* French Expeditionary Army
Slaves, first brought to Haiti, 10; number of, 11; slave ships, 12; cruelty toward, 12–13, 22; living conditions, 13; language, 14; described, 14, 16; relation with masters, 16–17. *See also* Maroons; Slavery; Voodoo
"Snake Gully," 154–56, 160
Social receptions, 122, 123
Sonthonax, 47–49, 50, 51–52, 53, 54, 55, 56, 62, 81–85, 96
Spanish, settle Haiti, 9–11; cede western third to France, 10–11; declare war on France, 43; Toussaint fights with, 44–47; alliance with England, 54–55; conquest of Haiti imminent, 55; Toussaint's victories against, 58, 59–60; peace treaty with France, 60, 61; and Louisiana Territory, 135, 136. *See also* Santo Domingo
Switzerland, 176

Tax, 116, 118
Theater, 17, 120

191

Toussaint Louverture. *See* Louverture, François Dominique Toussaint

Trade, exports, 5, 62, 117, 118; French monopoly of, 22, 79, 142; treaties with United States and British, 78-79, 90-91; free

Tribal warfare. *See* Guerrilla-warfare tactics

Tropical diseases, 162. *See also* Yellow fever

United States, Revolution of 1776, 21, 22, 64; fears British conquest of Haiti, 55; trade treaty with Toussaint, 78-79, 90-91; Toussaint rejects French scheme to invade, 90-91; Toussaint receives arms from, 130; Louisiana Territory, 135-36, 182; fears Napoleon's schemes, 136, 142, 182; Toussaint affects history of, 182

Vernet (mulatto general), 154
Villate (mulatto general), 65, 66, 67-68

Vincent (French general), 102-03, 122, 127-28, 129, 134-35

Voodoo, 27-28, 34, 37, 42, 119

War. *See* French Expeditionary Army; Slave Rebellion; War of the Knives

War of the Knives, 98-103, 107

Weapons. *See* Arms

West Indies, 9, 76, 162. *See also* Haiti; Guadeloupe; Jamaica

Whites, population, 19, 116; Little Whites, 19-20, 41; Big Whites, 19-20; relations with Toussaint, 62, 63-64, 68, 73-75, 83, 119, 122, 123, 128, 137-38, 165; response to French expedition, 137-38, 143; massacred, 183. *See also* Colonial Assembly; Creoles; Planters; specific nationalities

Yellow fever, 70, 71, 73, 165, 170, 174, 178